ASSISTED

DATE DUE

The Philosophica series covers works dealing with perennial questions of the history of philosophy. The series particularly seeks works written within the European Continental and the analytic traditions. In conformity with the Press's editorial policy, the series welcomes manuscripts written in either English or French.

Series Director: Josiane Ayoub

φ PHILOSOPHICA   Nº 51

ASSISTED SUICIDE

CANADIAN PERSPECTIVES

Edited by C. G. PRADO

Foreword by Margaret P. Battin
Preface by Anne Mullens

UNIVERSITY OF OTTAWA PRESS

University of Ottawa Press gratefully acknowledges the support extended to its publishing programme by the Canada Council and the University of Ottawa.

We acknowledge the financial support of the Government of Canada through the Book Publishing Industry Development Program for this project.

This book has been published with the help of a subvention from the Canadian Association for Publishing in Philosophy.

Canadian Cataloguing in Publication Data

Main entry under title:
  Assisted suicide: Canadian perspectives

(Philosophica; no. 51)
Includes bibliographical references.
ISBN 0-7766-0515-1

  1. Assisted suicide – Moral and ethical aspects – Canada. 2. Assisted suicide – Canada. I. Prado, C. G. II. Title. III. Series: Collection Philosophica; no. 51.

R726.A86 2000   179.7   C00-900281-2

 UNIVERSITY OF OTTAWA
UNIVERSITÉ D'OTTAWA

Cover Design: Robert Dolbec

ISBN 0-7766-0515-1
ISSN 1480-4670

Printed and bound in Canada

ACKNOWLEDGMENTS

———

My thanks to those who contributed to this collection, both for their articles and their patience through the always difficult process of publication. My thanks also to Alex Zieba for his productive suggestions on the Introduction and for the quotation that begins it. Special thanks to Karen Weteleinen, Ivana Dragicevic and Kajori Rahman, who worked as my research assistants updating Bronwyn Singleton's annotated bibliography ("The Media Perspective"). I am grateful to the Canadian Association for Publishing in Philosophy for a grant toward production costs.

———

CONTENTS

FOREWORD

Out here, in the rest of the world, we must greet the appearance of an "all-Canadian" volume on physician-assisted suicide with exceptional enthusiasm. It may be difficult to realize how important an *all-Canadian* contribution to the global discussion of assisted dying is, if one just thinks of Canada as a chilly, spread-out land that disappears on the north into arctic tundra, on the west to the remote Pacific rim, on the east into internecine tensions over language-groups and on the remaining, southern edge to a long, tough border with a 900-pound gorilla of a neighboring country. But Canada is an exceptional country—on many indices, one of the best in the world—and it is this fact that makes this collection about physician-assisted suicide so important.

To be sure, the fact that this collection is "all-Canadian" gives it particular relevance for a Canadian audience. The volume presents Canadian philosophers, Canadian physicians and Canadian legal theorists all talking with each other, among them some of the most distinguished voices in applied ethics that Canada—or the world—has to offer. There is a commonality of understanding in this volume; these authors understand Canada's urban and rural social patterns, its ethnic groupings, its economic conditions, its common-law legal structure and both the past and recent history and institutions of Canada's medical world: its regional health system, its history of nationalization, its arrangements for reimbursement and salaries for physicians, nurses and other health-care providers, and the structure of health insurance and coverage for all individual Canadians.

One might think that these common understandings would limit the interest of this volume to Canadians only. But, on the contrary, it is precisely these common understandings among a group of Canadian thinkers discussing sensitive issues about physician-assisted suicide that make this volume so important for the rest of the world. For it is these matters— social histories, ethnic relationships, economic conditions, legal structures and the practices and institutions of the medical world—upon which many of the contentions in such disputes, the practical premises, are based. The argument over assisted suicide is not a merely theoretical argument; it is a real-world argument, involving many factual, empirical claims. Everywhere in the world they are occurring, the disputes over physician-assisted suicide flare up as an argument between those who favor patient autonomy and personal choice, on the one hand, and those on the other hand who are concerned about the erosion of protections against killing and the so-called slippery slope. Of course, there are other concerns as well, including the avoidance of pain, the mandates of religious principle and the integrity of the medical profession. But I think the root tension in these disputes is between support for self-determination on the one hand and fear of abuse on the other. These applied-ethics issues are not merely philosophical; they are conditioned by the practical environment in which they take place.

It is precisely this that makes a *Canadian* discussion of these issues so important for an international audience. Canada is a country in which the practical conditions relevant to this dispute are, so to speak, at their best. Canada's English and French heritage gives it a legacy of Enlightenment respect for self-determination. Canada's more recent tradition of welcomed immigration and renewed respect for indigenous peoples has meant a tradition of respect for "minority" persons that is, while not perfect, as genuine as that anywhere in the world. Canada has a much greater degree of social and economic equality than many other countries, and hence is less subject to class-related tensions. Of course, Canada has problems over self-determination, particularly in friction over francophone secession in Quebec. But Canadian respect for self-determination, both for individuals and for an immense range of ethnic and racial groups, is still an admirable achievement, particularly when compared with the much greater degrees of racism and ethnic tension evident in many places in the world, including my own country, the 900-pound gorilla to Canada's south.

Canada's health-care situation is also distinctive, and, again, among the best. Canada offers all its citizens across-the-board, government-provided access to health care. It is particularly noteworthy that Canada offers access to health care at the same level for all. Its system is a one-tiered system, offering the same coverage to all residents—it is not dependent on the varying details of specific insurance plans, on a person's employment status and so on. This is not to say Canada's health system is perfect; there remain complaints about waiting lines, about the unavailability of some forms of high-tech diagnosis and treatment, about difficulties of access for groups in comparatively remote locations. Just the same, Canada comes among the closest to providing universal access to all health care for all persons of just about any country, with only a few, like the Netherlands and Sweden, vying for this crown. Furthermore, Canada's health system has one of the highest user-satisfaction ratings of any in the world.

These facts too are relevant to discussion of physician-assisted suicide. All Canadians are entitled to full health care and to hospice-style care. Physicians do not make more money or less money depending on whether they overtreat or undertreat a patient. Thus the person who is diagnosed with terminal illness, as the person seeking physician assistance in suicide is most likely to be, has access to full health care and pain control and does not constitute a financial advantage or disadvantage to the physician in whose care he or she finds him or herself. Because of these things, the Canadian patient facing death is, so to speak, better off—at least in theory—than practically any patient in the world. This, of course, does not mean that dying is easy for every Canadian patient. But the terminally ill Canadian, unlike the terminally ill resident of many other countries, lives in a culture with ample respect for self-determination, in a country that provides full access to health care, including pain control, and in a culture that is comparatively free of racism and other pressures against minorities.

Does this change the character of the assisted-suicide debate? To see, we need only open this volume. Is the appeal to self-determination we find in many of these authors subtly different than that in writing from some other countries, and if so, is that because respect for autonomy can be taken for granted, at least comparatively speaking? Are worries about the slippery slope, so severe in the United States for the uninsured and underinsured, muted here, and do concerns about financial incentives for physicians either in continuing burdensome treatment or terminating the lives of their patients play little or no role? Is there less distrust of government in manipulating health-care choices? Do concerns about risks to "vulnerable" patients have less purchase, too, in a culture in which differences of race, ethnic background, disability and so on may be less severe?

These are some of the questions for an international audience to explore in this Canadian volume. What is important is how the issue of physician-assisted suicide looks to a distinguished group of writers and theorists when their view is that from a country closer to "ideal" in many relevant respects than practically anywhere else in the world. What we can see here, subtle as these differences may be, is how assisted suicide is viewed where the background circumstances are, to so speak, "as good as it gets." This will tell us a great deal about the nature of the debate, and it will also tell us about what other less fortunate countries might aspire to achieve in responding to the situations of their dying patients.

Margaret P. Battin
October 1999
Author of *The Least Worst Death* and
The Death Debate: Ethical Issues in Suicide

PREFACE

In August of 1992, I drove out to an unassuming suburban house on the Saanich Peninsula north of Victoria. A tall, attractive woman, age 42, met me at the door. Except for a slightly unsteady gait and hint of a quaver in her voice, she seemed outwardly healthy; but she was dying. Her name was Sue Rodriguez and she had decided that summer to challenge the law that prohibited assisted suicide. I was the first journalist to interview her. We sat in the dappled shade of her backyard and talked about life and her approaching death from amyotrophic lateral sclerosis. As a mother with young children myself, it was impossible not to identify with her struggle. It was impossible not to ask: What would I want if I were in her situation?

Sue's determined battle to have an assisted suicide eventually captivated a nation and put a personal face on what had been largely a conceptual issue. It forced our society to begin looking at whether we can safely give an individual the right to ask for help in death without endangering the lives of others. Her situation was by no means an isolated one, but her decision to challenge the most powerful institutions in our land—the medical establishment, the government and the law—was almost mythic in proportions. Here was an ill and dying David taking on society's Goliaths.

Her fight, coinciding as it did with Dr. Jack Kevorkian's increasing activities in the United States, with referendums for assisted suicide in Oregon and Washington, with the first scientific studies on assisted deaths out of the Netherlands, built a momentum that will keep this issue on the forefront of medical, legal and societal concerns for decades to come.

And make no mistake—the questions of when we die and how our death occurs will inevitably become larger as years go by. There are five distinct trends pushing the growing debate over managed death: a rapidly aging population, an increase in patient autonomy and corresponding decline in medical paternalism, a growing disillusionment with medical management at the end of life, a century-long rise in individualism and a decline in religious belief. All these forces are coming together and will determine whether we, as a society, are able to allow choices in death to become an even more dominant conundrum in the future.

First, however, to deal with these issues, we need to be able to talk about them. The essays collected in this book will help in defining the territory for discussion. It is a vast landscape that is impossible to cover in a single volume. Law, medicine, ethics, religion, philosophy, sociology, psychology, history, public opinion and public policy all play a role in whether individuals should be allowed to ask someone else to help them die. In this collection we are fortunate to be able to look at the issues through the experience and reasoning of clinicians, legal experts, philosophers and ethicists. One of the more unique contributions in this book is the annotated bibliography of all the major articles on assisted suicide and euthanasia that appeared in three prominent newspapers over the last decade.[1] To read it is to witness firsthand a time-lapse picture of an issue in evolution.

In the years ahead, some of the debate over managed death will be illuminated by the experiences in a few pioneering jurisdictions. For 20 years, the Netherlands has been leading the experiment. Now Oregon and Australia's Northern Territories will offer other examples about whether choices in death can be safely managed and controlled without putting the lives of vulnerable people at risk and without changing society in ways the majority regrets.

The challenge for social scientists will be to assess these unique situations fairly, and honestly, without the blinkers of ideology. As the Netherlands has shown, those looking for evidence of abuse will find it and those looking for confirmation that the policy is working beautifully will find it, too. As a journalist who studied the Netherlands in depth, I found the truth lies somewhere in-between. The elderly are not afraid. Pain control and care of the dying can rival any Western nation and a wide range of choices, including British-style palliative care, are increasingly available. Yet two national studies have shown the guidelines for assisted death sometimes are not strictly followed and some doctors, out of the paternalistic belief they know what the patient would have wanted, have acknowledged ending a dying patient's life without a specific request. Only time will tell whether the Dutch are, as some claim, sliding down the slippery slope, or in fact, slowly climbing up that slope, using prosecuted cases that lie at the margins of acceptable behavior as the pitons that fix and clarify regulations, and finding a secure and ethical place on that slope to bivouac.

As this collection aptly points out, one of the persistent stumbling blocks in the debate is semantics. Often similar actions are called different names, and highly dissimilar actions are called the same thing. This shifting ground and inability to agree on terms feeds the continual polarization and obfuscation of the issues.

The debate over euthanasia and assisted suicide boils down to the classic dilemma of an individual's rights versus the perceived needs of the state. It asks a number of profound questions: Do individuals have the right to control the circumstances of their death or should that be left to God or nature? What is the role of government in enforcing public morality or in accommodating moral choice? Can we devise a legislative system that respects individual autonomy yet at the same time protects those less able to exercise their autonomy, such as the disabled, the disadvantaged, the elderly or the depressed? Can we honor the right to die without subtly creating the obligation to die? These questions and more add complexity to a debate that is becoming more divisive than the abortion debate. Indeed, while much of the 20th century featured a struggle to work through reproductive rights, the next century will shift the focus to the control of the timing and manner of death.

The mere mention of the word "death" makes many people uncomfortable, but death for all of us is inevitable. Through the discussions and debate fostered by collections like this, we are helped in our ability to confront and accept the inevitability of death. It is one more step on this voyage of discovery.

Anne Mullens
October 1999
Author of *Timely Death: Considering Our Last Rights*

1. Editor's note: Every effort was made by Ms. Bronwyn Singleton and the researchers who compiled the annotated bibliography to include all the articles appearing in relevant newspapers in the periods covered. However, while certainly representative, the annotated bibliography is not offered as exhaustive.

C. G. Prado

INTRODUCTION

Nunc lento sonitu dicunt, morieris
(Now this bell tolling softly for another, says to me,
Thou must die)

———

A sea change is taking place in our attitude toward death. Death has come out of the closet. More accurately, *dying* is being increasingly acknowledged as an integral part of human life, as was the norm prior to our century's hygienic isolation of death. Dying has ceased to be something fearfully unspoken and, in reversion to earlier times, involves the community both as an event and an issue. In particular, our attitude toward death has changed with the need for reflection and planning about how we die beyond the financial and funerary arrangements necessitated by death itself.

A major cause of the change in attitude toward dying is the increasing capacity to sustain life by the application of technology. Medicine's new power to stretch out the time it takes to die forces historically novel decisions on people whose lives are ending. When it became possible to extend the process of dying, it became necessary to make decisions about when to stop doing so. Protraction of death prompted a good deal of thought about the wisdom of delaying the inevitable at great personal, familial and social cost and generated much talk about "dying with dignity" and "the right to die." As a consequence, many reject the protraction of dying beyond a point at which living becomes mere survival.

However, the protraction of dying is a highly technical process, and decisions to stop that process can't be enacted by

the patient alone. Enacting a decision to stop life's technological maintenance almost invariably involves the participation
of those whose expert efforts pose the need for the decision in
the first place. The result is that patients who choose not to
have their lives technologically maintained, or to accelerate
the deaths entailed by terminal illness, embroil their doctors
in their decision. This practically inescapable embroilment
produced the historically new idea of *physician-assisted suicide*, that is, the decision made by incapacitated individuals
who are under medical care not to live under certain conditions, a decision that requires the help of their attending physicians to carry out the chosen course of action. However, for
physicians to actively involve themselves in the deaths of patients in their care is to violate, or at least to challenge, professional principles and traditions, social trust and legal
interdictions.

Taking one's own life is still criminal in only a few places,[1]
but helping someone else to die is proscribed in most jurisdictions. Despite the decriminalization of suicide, *assisting*
suicide is classed with performing euthanasia as forms of culpable homicide. Though judges and juries may ultimately
temper the consequences of violating the proscription, in the
first instance someone who assists in suicide is chargeable
with murder or manslaughter. While this is the status quo
with very few exceptions,[2] special situations produced by the
medical protraction of dying have made many accept the view
that "managing"[3] the deaths of terminal patients must be allowed. The result is that we've been debating for some time
about decriminalizing the helping to die of some who *want* to
die and who have *good reason* to want to die. Unfortunately,
the debate has grown in scope and intensity without making
proportionate progress.

Proponents of managed death think of the application of
medical technology as only postponing imminent death. Thus
stopping the application of that technology is not seen as advancing death but as ceasing to prevent its "natural" occurrence. Delaying death is seen as gaining borrowed time, so
ceasing to delay death isn't seen as *killing*, but as not continu-

ing to artificially maintain life when doing so becomes harm-
ful. Hastening death in terminal illness is more contentious,
but in both cases the position is essentially utilitarian. That is,
life is considered renounceable if the interests of the individual are best served by avoiding pointless suffering.

Against this, opponents see medical technology as having
established a new temporal horizon for human life. They see
patients as not only having a right to technologically gained
time, but an obligation to avail themselves of that time. That
right and that obligation are seen as following on life's unique
and ultimate value. The possibility of preserving life is taken
to entail its preservation, so for their part, physicians are perceived as obliged to employ the relevant technology. Patients'
requests that they not do so then are construed as the effects
of depression and perhaps inadequate palliative care. In this
view, stopping the application of technology is reprehensible
killing, however compassionate the motives may be. Hastening death in terminal illness is seen as murder or self-murder
and so as unjustified. The position is essentially deontological
in the sense that life is judged unrenounceable because the
consequences of suicide or euthanasia, however desired, don't
justify killing.

The moral gulf between conceptions of life as renounceable and unrenounceable is profound. As with the abortion
debate, the managed-death debate almost certainly will continue fundamentally unresolved. Recognizing this, many proponents and opponents strive not for resolution but for
political and legislative dominance. Those who genuinely
want to achieve a more lasting resolution must begin by appreciating that more is involved in the debate than two opposed and intractable conceptions of human life. Noting the
difference between perception of managed death as relin-
quishment of something not really one's own, or as abandon-
ment of something one has an obligation to preserve, is only a
beginning. It is important to understand the specific forms
these perceptions take in the managed-death debate. The key
to this understanding is recognizing that while individual participants in the debate have their respective positions and

varying impacts on the debate, it is the members of the various professions involved who define the issue of managed death and give the debate its direction. This is not always seen. There is a tendency to take advocacy of or opposition to managed death as a consequence of an individuals' basic moral views on whether hastening or deliberately not delaying death is or is not permissible. When proponents and opponents of managed death are seen as taking sides on the question for personal moral reasons, the importance of their professional affiliations is underestimated. Those affiliations are acknowledged as significant, because they determine how individuals actually come into contact with cases of managed death, but are seen as of secondary importance. Moral views and commitments are assumed to be prior to those affiliations. That's very often a mistake, because prior moral commitments are heavily conditioned and oriented by prior training, professional responsibilities and day-to-day experience.

In appreciating the effects of training, professional responsibilities and experiences on moral stands on managed death, the most important distinction to draw is between people whose views on managed death are, in fact, determined mainly by their moral beliefs, and people whose views are determined by how their professional background and practice influence, qualify and mold their moral beliefs. Training and day-to-day work experience make a crucial difference to how general moral beliefs are actually focused and applied, and to what in particular is and is not construed as raising moral questions.

We are all familiar with how the general public often is dismayed and even shocked at what they perceive as callousness or insensitivity in how some professionals deal with cases and situations. The most notorious such instances involve the police, but emergency-ward staff often come in for harsh criticism for what people who are unfamiliar with dealing with life-threatening trauma sometimes see as uncaring coolness or unconcerned implementation of routine procedures. Most of the cases drawing attention may be extreme ones, but it is undeniable that those who deal daily with actual and impending death in a medical context cannot help but be somewhat inured against death's gravity, and are bound to develop somewhat different perceptions of what poses a moral issue regarding the end of moribund life. The other side of inurement is compassion augmented by expert knowledge. Physicians familiar with what dying patients face also may develop different perceptions of what poses a moral issue regarding death when the alternative is life of a blighted and tenuous nature. Either because of a hardening toward death, or heightened feeling for suffering, physicians may perceive the moral import of certain actions regarding the hastening or not delaying of death as blunted and even as of dubious relevance. Their perceptions, though, then may be at odds with those of laypeople.

A second, powerful consideration is that physicians' judgments are constrained by professional ethics that differ from broader cultural and, for some, universal codes of conduct in dealing with specific fiduciary responsibilities, duties and obligations. But however precise the codes, there is always a margin for interpretation, and different attitudes may make a very considerable difference in how those codes are applied. Perhaps the best example here is that most professional ethics support the common conception of doctors as healers, and to a large extent the equally common assumption that, as healers, doctors must always do all in their power to sustain life. Many physicians share this view, and consider that not doing all they can to sustain life is to fail in their mission. But as many, or more, understand that sometimes healing must be understood more broadly, and that alleviating suffering may require *not* sustaining life. Certain actions, then, might appear to laypeople as falling short of fulfillment of obligations, or even as reprehensible indifference, but be perceived by the physicians in question as best satisfying their duties to their patients.

We next have to distinguish among those whose professional involvement with managed death is direct or indirect. The key difference is between people actively engaged in the treatment of the dying, and people concerned with the governance of that treatment. Those engaged in treating the dying are clinicians of various kinds, though it is basically physicians who bear the major responsibility for treatment decisions. So long as we don't take the designation too rigidly, we can gloss the standpoints of physicians and other health-care workers as the "clinical" perspective. And because hospital and other institutional administrators are concerned with the governance of medical practice, not at the level of public policy, their standpoint is best included in the clinical perspective.

Those concerned with the broader governance of what clinicians do fall into two groups. The first includes philosophers and theologians; the second includes judges, lawyers, legislators and even jurors serving in precedent-setting cases. Essentially, members of the former group are concerned with the fundamental principles relevant to life-and-death decisions, while members of the latter group are concerned with the application of those principles in the regulation of clinical practices. Again not taking the designations too rigidly, we can dub the standpoints of these two groups the "philosophical" and the "juridical" perspectives.

The importance of distinguishing among the clinical, juridical and philosophical perspectives is that each supports a different conception of the nature of managed death *as an issue*, as well as influences how that issue is dealt with and what counts as its resolution. Depending on whether one deals directly with the dying, with the control and regulation of how the dying are treated or with the principles underlying that regulation, the tendency is to see managed death as either a professionally circumscribed medical issue, a precedent-setting social issue or an issue about our highest principles and our understanding of them.

The clinical perspective is shaped by the interplay of commitment to the tenets definitive of the practice of medicine, compassion and practical limitations. Conceptions of medical practice as a healing art and of physicians as preservers of life vie with the realization that some patients would be better off dying and realism about the efficacy of treatment and inevitable budgetary constraints. Physicians' perception of the permissibility of managed death is determined by their assessments of patients' needs, prospects and competence, by compassion for individuals in their care, by how they conceive their role as doctors, by institutional rules and requirements and by established personal and team practices for dealing with the messy details of individual cases.

Social and legal requirements and expectations shape the juridical perspective. Constitutional and statutory demands and precedents are paramount, as is the question of what "flows from" the sanctioning of a practice for society at large. Judges, lawyers and legislators assess the permissibility of managed death in terms of conformity to established law and the broader consequences of condoning or proscribing its provision.

Philosophers approach managed death in terms of principles and prevailing beliefs about the nature of right action, human agency, responsibility and autonomy. The philosophical perspective is shaped by moral and conceptual factors such as the nature and priority of autonomy and whether deontological or consequentialist principles should govern the disposition of life, that is, whether right action regarding elective death is determined by considerations of duty or by the desirability of its outcome.

The upshot of these perspectival differences is that physicians tend to see managed death as a *medical* and *ethical* issue, jurists tend to see managed death as a *social* and *legal* issue and philosophers tend to see managed death as a *moral* and *conceptual* issue. Prognoses, suffering, the effectiveness of treatment and accordance with professional ethical codes are the central considerations for physicians in making decisions about managing patients' deaths. For jurists the central considerations are compliance with existing law and what may be entailed for the general population by condoning the practice of managing death. For philosophers the central considerations are whether moral principles allow death to be hastened or not delayed where it is possible to delay it, and the precise nature and rationality of such acts as choosing to die or to not have life sustained and participating benevolently in another's death.

Once one sketches the differences among the philosophical, clinical and juridical perspectives, it immediately becomes clear that something is missing. The managed death debate involves at least one other pivotally important point of view having significant influence on the direction and, to a certain extent, the nature of the debate. In our time, little of note happens that isn't mirrored in, and to a considerable degree influenced by, the media. The media plays a crucial role in providing coverage of the debate and the cases that generate it by how it presents that coverage. Media treatment of the debate and relevant cases has a powerful effect. This is especially true of the press, in the case of the managed-death issue, because it is in major newspapers and magazines that we find coverage of managed death that is substantial enough to have real impact. But the point is that coverage of these developments is not a simple matter of conveying information to the public. Editors and journalists contribute to directing the debate by how they select and present news about the debate and its object-cases and projections.[4]

However, contrary to common opinion, the media's influence is not unilateral. While its influence is undeniable, and though it does its share of forming public perceptions and opinion, the media also does its share of following public opinion and perceptions. Editors' selection of what to cover and what to ignore, and reporters' approaches to news, are driven by sensitivity to the public's interests and expectations. An indication of this is how coverage of the managed-death debate has been surprisingly even-handed. The reason is that up to now it has been difficult to discern decisive public support for or against managed death. And reciprocally, that even-handed coverage has helped to temper many people's responses to the issue. However, things could change. If there were a clear-cut swing of public sentiment in favor of or against managed death, the emphasis in media coverage undoubtedly would shift either to accenting the preservation of dignity and prevention of suffering gained by the practice, or to stressing the violation of personal rights and the pernicious influence of cost-cutting in health care. Such shifts in pro or con accentuation in coverage are vitally important because of the effect they have on an electorate that must decide policy on managed death through referenda and support of or opposition to proposed and even enacted legislation.

As is always the case with complex issues, after distinguishing among the perspectives described, it becomes immediately important to introduce qualifications. The articles that follow amply show that few people who reflect seriously on the issue of managed death stay neatly in one or another of the professional groups characterized by the philosophical, juridical, clinical and media perspectives. For physicians, jurists in the broad sense defined or philosophers to think deeply about managed death, they invariably need to delve into each other's fields. Philosophers have to make juridical and clinical points; jurists need to tackle clinical and philosophical concepts and issues; clinicians find themselves inexorably drawn into philosophical and juridical controversies. Much of this is also true of those reporting on the managed death debate. For one thing, despite their need to remain as objective as possible, most of those who devote considerable time to covering the issue cannot help but delve a little into clinical, legal and philosophical questions. They have to know the subject matter they are covering well enough to report on it intelligently.

* * *

The essays collected in this book separately contribute to the debate on managed death, but the primary aim in bringing them together is to illustrate how different professional perspectives on the issue of managed death determine the nature and priority of questions posed and how they are addressed. A look at the list of contributors will provide information about their training and primary occupations, but it is amply clear in the essays how professional focus shapes the main concerns and approach of each author.

In an intensely personal piece, Wesley Boston reviews salient decisions and events in his experience as a palliative care physician, and how those decisions and events look from a point of view more informed by both philosophical reflection and recent discussion of medical practice regarding end-of-life issues. Boston provides an informative glimpse of what it is like to be involved in deciding how a person's life might best end, and how the decisions taken in the circumstances remain with one regardless of when they are enacted. Some understanding of the perspective of physicians immediately involved in managing death is absolutely necessary for abstract consideration and discussion of managed death to be productive. Boston's article also provides us with some grasp of the consequences to physicians themselves of dealing with dying patients. But perhaps most important is that the article poses the fundamental question of what the theoretician may offer the clinician to contribute to the better understanding and making of the hard decisions Boston wrestled with as a palliative care physician.

The next three essays attempt to define what is at issue in the managed-death debate. Jan Narveson's article raises the often ignored question about the extent to which we can separate definitional and substantial moral issues when confronting a problem as complex and consequential as the permissibility of helping people to die. What emerges is that drawing the distinctions we need to draw, for legal and professional ethics reasons, is all mixed up with how our moral presuppositions shape our perceptions of the very acts we want to differentiate.

Sandra Taylor's contribution focuses on accepted definitions and descriptions of what goes on in hospitals and on how clinicians conceive and represent their day-to-day practices regarding treatment and non-treatment of terminal patients. Her main concern is how present medical descriptive conventions obscure the nature of actual practice by characterizing cases of assisted suicide and euthanasia as instances of merely withholding or not initiating treatment. Most clinicians cling to an ultimately unworkable distinction between

tolerated and even promoted passive "letting die" and proscribed assistance in suicide or performance of euthanasia.

In my own article I address the matter of how debate
about managed death is usually and often facilely discussed in
terms of "assisted suicide." This won't do, because character-
ization of managed death as (assisted) suicide puts the moral
onus on the patients whose deaths are "managed" and tends
unwarrantedly to ameliorate the moral responsibilities of the
physicians who manage those deaths. Suicide may be rational
when done freely and for good enough reason,[5] but it is a real
and pressing question to determine who bears the main responsibility in cases where someone *else* is involved in its putative commission.

Russell Savage's and Eike-Henner Kluge's contributions
focus on the legal aspect of the managed-death debate, though
in different ways. Savage, writing as a Crown prosecutor, addresses the question of who may be "party" to managed death.
This is a key question regarding proper apportionment of legal
culpability, but how it is answered also has important implications with respect to our construal of involvement in managed death and our assessment of moral responsibility. Our
legal definitions of who is and is not party to a managed death
reflect our moral assessments of degree of involvement in
such a death; those definitions, in their application and development, also influence moral assessment. In the legal context
we find a fairly well defined idea of responsible participation,
one honed by court debate and judicial reasoning. That idea
serves us well as a reference point of contrast to better understand moral responsibility. The idea both encapsulates what
we have thought about the morality and permissibility of one
person's benevolent participation in causing another's death,
and enables informed adjustment to what we may think about
such participation now and in the future.

Writing as a philosopher deeply embroiled in a celebrated
case of "assisted suicide," Kluge's aim is to show why the section of the Criminal Code of Canada prohibiting assisted suicide should be changed. He feels the relevant section violates

three ethical principles fundamental to a democratic society. These principles are those of autonomy and respect for persons, of equality and justice and of beneficence. Kluge relates his consideration of how the section in question curtails or negates these principles to the Sue Rodriguez case, in which he played an important role. What he proposes is changes that would at once prevent violation of the principles he considers and prevent unscrupulous persons from taking advantage of the resulting legislation.

Where Savage's article illustrates the perspective on managed death of a philosophically trained lawyer, Kluge's illustrates that of a philosopher who is legally knowledgeable and has firsthand experience of how the courts deal with cases of assisted suicide and other forms of managed death.

David Checkland and Michel Silberfeld offer still another viewpoint on the managed-death issue. Melding diverse backgrounds and work-a-day experience, they address the matter of the role that decision-making capacity plays in "assisted suicide" or managed death. The authors press for a new sub-discipline concerned with assessing decisional capacity regarding managed death. They offer four criteria for discerning the specific capacity to make decisions about assisted suicide though they grant more criteria may be necessary. The authors also consider the question whether incompetent requests for assisted suicide should ever be honored. Given their respective backgrounds, Checkland and Silberfeld's essay complements Kluge's. Both articles illustrate how philosophical, professional and contextual factors must be carefully interwoven to advance our understanding of managed death and to sharpen our sensitivity to when it is permissible.

Representing the perspective of the media and of the press in particular, which has offered by far the greatest coverage of managed death, initially posed a problem. I approached a number of journalists who cover the managed-death debate. All were extremely busy and unable or reluctant to commit themselves to contributing a piece to this collection. Perhaps more important than schedule problems was that they were reluctant to generalize about media coverage and to write about views and practices other than their own. They also felt constrained to protect their professional credibility by not appearing to take sides on the issue.[6] But an article by someone who observes and studies the media in general or the press in particular seemed rather to miss the point. My objective was to *illustrate* press coverage in order to suggest how it has helped to shape the managed-death debate. I was not looking for analysis of the influence of the press from a more abstract point of view. The latter necessitates taking a particular theoretical standpoint, and that means the resulting article in effect would be once removed in that it would provide a perspective on the media's perspective.

The solution presented itself as an annotated bibliography of recent and representative articles on managed death. Bronwyn Singleton lists and briefly describes a substantial number of articles on "assisted suicide" that appeared in three of North America's most widely read newspapers, *The Globe and Mail*, the *National Post* and *The New York Times*. In this way, the media perspective is effectively illustrated, and some idea of its impact on the nature and direction of the managed-death debate is provided. Also, by ordering the various articles by date, from most recent to earliest, the list conveys the way in which press coverage of managed death increased dramatically just prior to and after the U.S. Supreme Court decision of 1997.

A great deal has been and is being written about managed death or "assisted suicide." There is no question that our society is in the process of establishing new standards and practices regarding death management. The consequences of doing so could be good or they could be horrendous. The crucial point is that nothing of the order of magnitude of this sort of moral, legal and social change can be undone quickly. If things go wrong, many will die prematurely before problems are recognized, much less fixed. The following articles may not provide firm answers; none of the contributors would aspire to that. But the articles do present the more salient issues that need our attention if we are going to consider managed death productively and enact sound legislation regarding its practice. We cannot, each of us, hope adequately to cover the many facets of the managed-death issue. This collection is not offered as a way for readers to take positions on the facets discussed; it is offered with the expectation that the articles will open readers' eyes to facets they may not have considered with the attention those facets deserve.

C. G. Prado
October 1999

1. Attempted suicide and suicide are not illegal in most North American and European jurisdictions. Germany decriminalized suicide as early as 1751, Canada as late as 1972.

2. For example, Oregon.

3. I do not like the term "managed death," but it has the advantage of being more neutral than the alternatives. The favored term, "assisted suicide," is either a misnomer or a term of art the sense of which is still being defined.

4. A case in point is the presentation of violent crime in the media, which tends to be somewhat alarmist in both emphasis and extent of coverage. Media coverage of violent crime has prompted movements to toughen laws and sentencing and often heavily influence legislation. What is noteworthy is that this is so despite the fact that violent crime actually has been declining for the past six years. Ironically, this fact has itself been reported in the press. See John Cushman, "Serious Crime in U.S. Fell in 1997 for a 6th Year," *The New York Times*, May 18, 1998.

5. Prado, 1990, 1998.

6. I am very grateful to several reporters who took the time to correspond with or speak to me about this project. I especially want to mention Sheryl Gay Stolberg, Peter Steinfels, Linda Greenhouse and Gina Kolata, all at *The New York Times*, and Jane Coutts at *The Globe and Mail* in Toronto.

Robert Wesley Boston

CROSSING THE LINE

A Reflection on Palliative Care and Assisted Suicide[1]

───────

Throughout most of Western history death has occurred at home. Only the indigent were taken to hospital to die, but in the second half of the 20th century things changed. Spurred by the exigencies of the Second World War and by the postwar surge of energy and affluence, the 1950's and 60's saw scientific medicine take a great leap forward. Among its accomplishments were the development of antibiotics, safer anesthetics and surgical techniques for treatment of heretofore inoperable disease. Instead of places of last resort, hospitals became places of hope, for cure and of promise for longer life. The center of scientific medicine moved from home and clinic to hospital, but with this shift death also moved from home to hospital. When curative treatment was no longer effective for patients in hospital, and when "nothing more could be done" for them, they were transferred either to the little side rooms of British wards or, in North America, to rooms furthest removed from the nursing station; and there they languished. Astute observers of what was happening wrote brilliantly about this shift of death from home to hospital— among them psychiatrists John Hinton in Britain[2] and Elisabeth Kübler-Ross in North America.[3]

A most memorable passage from Hinton's writings is this: "They (the nurses) emerge with far greater credit than we, who are capable of ignoring the conditions which make muted

───────

people suffer. The dissatisfied dead cannot noise abroad the negligence they have experienced."[4] One such British nurse, who had also trained as a social worker, was Cicely Saunders.[5] Strongly motivated to improve the care of patients dying in hospital, she "swatted up medicine" so that she might confront, on its own turf, the medical establishment so neglectful of these patients. Her pioneering work in symptom control in terminal illness, and her founding of St. Christopher's Hospice in Sydenham, England,[6] set the stage for the development of modern palliative medicine. Dr. Saunders (later Dame Cicely Saunders) is now acknowledged as the founder of the modern hospice movement.[7] Today, palliative medicine is a discipline with scientific standards as demanding as those for curative medicine, but with a philosophy of treatment that accepts the inevitability of death, and which aims "to add life to days rather than just days to life."[8] This new medical specialty has gained formal recognition in several countries, and the movement has spread worldwide with one notable exception—the Netherlands. In that country voluntary euthanasia and/or assisted suicide has been championed as the alternative to the protracted suffering of a terminal illness.

About the same time as Saunders was beginning to challenge the British medical establishment on how to care for dying patients isolated in the side rooms of their great wards, I was a junior intern on a Canadian Department of Veterans' Affairs ward to which an elderly veteran, dying of stomach cancer, had been admitted. He was assigned the room furthest from the nursing station, very small and half underground. There, this wasted man with his large stomach tumor lived out his last days. On rounds, the august head of the teaching team would inquire of the dying man and then turn the team around before it reached his room. Undoubtedly that memory, after a quarter century as a neonatologist caring for sick and premature infants at the beginning of life, was one of the influences that nudged me toward a year of retraining in palliative medicine and, in turn, led to a very rewarding nine years of palliative medicine practice in hospital and community.

As a clinician having struggled with ethical issues surrounding both the first breath and the last, I came to retirement with a wish to understand better the ethical principles that I believed had guided my practice. I took up philosophy. In this essay, drawing on my experience as a palliative care clinician, I try to examine with the rigor of philosophy and the honesty of retirement, those principles that, in my mind, kept me from crossing the line that separates aggressive action to control symptoms in terminal illness from action designed to relieve suffering by hastening death.

The March 9, 1998 issue of *Maclean's* magazine[9] provides a graphic account of why the first-degree murder charge against Halifax respirologist Dr. Nancy Morrison was dismissed. Her patient was a 65-year-old man who, within seven months, had undergone 10 operations for esophageal cancer. He had an incurable chest infection and was ventilator-dependent. He was clearly near the end of his life. At 12:30 p.m. on November 10, 1996, after discussions with family, his ventilator support was withdrawn. To ease the patient's suffering, his already large dose of opiate was massively increased. It failed to control his anguished gasping for air, described by his experienced bedside Intensive Care Unit nurse as "a horrible and hideous scene." The murder charge was based upon an alleged intravenous bolus injection of potassium chloride by Dr. Morrison just before the patient died at 2:59 p.m.

Potassium chloride is of no value in relief of pain or gasping; but it is well known, in bolus doses, to stop the heart. In court the patient's bedside nurse described herself as "completely stunned by the events that transpired that afternoon." It also was reported in court that when the nursing supervisor asked Dr. Morrison why she had administered potassium chloride, she replied: "Oh my God, I don't know why." In the murder trial the Crown attempted to prove that Dr. Morrison had crossed a clear ethical boundary. The presiding judge, not convinced that a legal boundary had been crossed, dismissed the charge. The Crown challenged the dismissal by resorting to a rarely used provision—a preferred indictment—on the lesser charge of manslaughter. Finally, the Nova Scotia Attorney

General, responding to public pleas that the case against Dr. Morrison be dropped,[10] stated that "We want to look at whether there should be another classification within the Criminal Code that would allow for compassion" and that "The issues surrounding the end of life are very difficult, they're very emotional...and we need better guidelines."

In his lecture notes on symptom control in terminal cancer, Dr. Robert Twycross writes:

All treatment has inherent risk

It is axiomatic that, even in extreme situations, the least drastic remedy should be employed. If physical or mental distress is considered to be intolerable and intractable, the least drastic remedy is to render the patient unconscious, not to kill him.

Prognostication is an art, not a science

The possibility of unexpected recovery must not be ignored. Except when death is likely within a few hours or days, the potential for improvement should not be substantially lessened by the treatment prescribed.[11]

In these succinct headings and sentences, Dr. Twycross captures well the essence of the *line* of ethical behavior that a palliative care clinician feels bound not to cross. But the remarks raise a number of questions. What ethical principle or principles support this practical advice? In its application, is the line drawn always clear, or is it sometimes blurred or indistinct? Could it ever be "in the patient's best interest" to skirt or ignore this advice, that is, to cross the line?

Throughout my busy years of palliative care practice, I felt comfortably assured that never once had I crossed this line; but on a few occasions I was hard pressed to know where the line was, and on a few others sorely tempted to cross it. One day in the earlier years of my practice, I was summoned urgently to the hospital room of a patient who had been admitted within that hour in extreme respiratory distress. I had not encountered her before, but a hurried perusal of her chart revealed ample documentation of advanced cancer, metastatic to the lungs. She had had several recent admissions for treatment of severe shortness of breath. What I saw when I entered the small, hot room in an older part of the hospital was a frail, wasted woman, propped almost vertical, receiving high-flow oxygen by mask and gasping desperately for every breath. It was the worst dyspnea crisis I had ever seen; but what made it so bad was that she was fully conscious and wide-eyed with fright, and between gasps she pleaded for something to relieve her distress. Her husband, standing beside her, echoed her pleas. I knew I faced a real crisis.

I took the husband into the corridor, and I am certain that in my opening remarks I conveyed to him my distress and my compassion for the desperate plight of his wife. It was evident from the brief exchange that he had walked very closely with his wife through the months of her terminal illness. I told him that I could give medication to his wife that would relieve her extreme distress, but that it was a very fine line that separated relieving her symptoms from causing her death; perhaps she might die. Despite this warning, without hesitation, he urged me to try to relieve his wife's extreme suffering. In a few moments, with essential help from a very supportive nurse, I had a needle in the woman's vein and began to inject—ever so slowly—first opiate and then anxiolytic. I had done this before, and was to do it a number of times again; but this experience was unique, and remains distressingly vivid in my memory. As I injected slowly over minutes, the woman's extremely labored breathing became less so. She gradually relaxed and drifted into what seemed like a light sleep. Nurse, husband and I, breathing more easily, waited. What made this experience unique was what happened over the next 15 to 20 minutes. The woman's respiratory rate and effort continued to decrease, gradually, slowly, not leveling out as I was expecting, but progressed to a final breath, to death. The line between relieving her extreme dyspnea and causing her death had indeed been very fine. Most fortunate for me, the coroner took a charitable view of what I had done. The patient's death was attributed to natural causes. I was able to continue in the rich and rewarding practice of palliative medicine, sadder and wiser for the experience.

Several examples of being tempted, like Dr. Morrison, to cross the line come readily to mind. One will suffice. A certain patient once had been my teacher, a brilliant, creative and fiercely independent man who now had become a shadow of his former self, diminished by multisystem disease, including intractable congestive heart failure and a stroke that had left him with a somewhat incapacitating hemiplegia. However, his mind was as sharp as ever, his speech unimpaired. On my first encounter with him, as his physician, he expressed his desire for assistance in bringing his life to a quick end. Although stretched by this request from a teacher whom I admired, I confidently responded that I could not provide that assistance, but that I could, and with his permission, would walk with him through his last days of living, and that there were things to be done to make those days more tolerable. To anticipate C. G. Prado and S. J. Taylor, I agreed that these could become days in which value could still be added to my teacher's life.[12]

As it turned out my teacher did have several months of quality living; and then, as a colleague used to say, all the wheels came off. In a few days he went from wheelchair mobility to confinement to bed, with massive swelling of his body (fluid retention), incontinence and vomiting. On the last day of his life came the worst possible complication—a massive stomach hemorrhage, with aspiration of vomited blood into his lungs, causing severe respiratory distress. In the hour or so before he lapsed into unconsciousness, he raised himself up, looked me squarely in the eye, and with penetrating forcefulness, said: "Dr. Boston, you never told me it would be this bad!" I wanted so very much to end the suffering of my teacher and colleague. Yet something held me back from sparing him the final hour or so of his terminal agony.

In their *Assisted Suicide: Theory and Practice in Elective Death*, Prado and Taylor provide a penetrating analysis of "end of life" issues, and offer ethical guidelines for assisted suicide, which they describe as "an idea whose time has come, despite many questions and problems." Drawing on Prado and Taylor, as well as nine years experience in the practice of palliative medicine, I attempt in what follows to define, if only for myself, the ethical line that Dr. Morrison was accused of crossing and that I was, on occasion, tempted to cross but felt

I never did. I also ask whether, in light of the insights provided by Prado and Taylor, and others, I could bring myself to cross that line. Put another way, the primary question addressed here is whether a serious commitment to the principles of modern palliative care is compatible with a willingness to provide compassionate assistance in the commission of suicide. What impact might such a willingness have on palliative care clinicians, the palliative care movement, and "slippery slope" arguments against assisted suicide and compassionate voluntary euthanasia?

Prado and Taylor focus on the "assisted suicide" component of debate about end of life issues. They view assisted suicide as a present reality that demands well thought out ethical guidelines. They argue passionately that practical guidelines must be founded upon general ethical principles, but also point out that much of the confusion in the death debate stems from conflicts regarding such principles. At the heart of the philosophical conflict is, on the one hand, the belief attributed to theologian Thomas Aquinas that life is an unrenounceable gift from our Creator, of which we are the responsible custodians; and, on the other hand, the view espoused by philosopher David Hume that life is a disposable possession over which we may, with discretion, exercise our free will or autonomy. Intuitively, there seems to be truth in both positions, but in fact they are irreconcilable, and in the crunch one must be chosen over the other.

The principles by which we choose to live and die are very much influenced by religious upbringing (or lack thereof), by life experiences and by education and intellectual inquiry. Serious debate about the morality of assisted suicide or voluntary euthanasia reaches an apparent impasse at staunch ideological adherence to the principle that life is an unrenounceable gift, and not a disposable possession. If we accept that life is a possession about which we can make choices, then the primary question becomes: Is suicide or assisted suicide ever rational? Only if the answer is yes can the morality of suicide and assisted suicide be debated, for only rational acts can be morally culpable.

Arguing against the prevailing view of the late-19th and 20th centuries that suicide is always irrational, Prado and Taylor state that suicide *can* be both rational and moral and offer criteria by which to judge whether or not a suicide—and, by extension, assistance with a suicide—is rational. A critically important assumption underlying these criteria is that suicide must always be an autonomous act, that is, a decision made freely, knowingly and resolutely. The three criteria in briefest summary hold that to be rational,

1) suicide must present itself as a real option, and the reasoning leading to the suicidal decision must be unimpaired by error, false beliefs or lack of relevant information;

2) a potential suicidist's motives for self-destruction must make good sense to others, and not unduly contravene the agent's perceived interests; and

3) suicide must benefit the individual more than continuing to live; that is, it must be in the agent's best interests.[13]

The main problem posed by these criteria is in their interpretation and application to the specific circumstances of clinical practice. It is in this attempt to apply general philosophical principles to the messy contours of a terminal illness, to apply logic to a situation that often seems to defy logic, that a serious gulf between theorist and clinician becomes apparent. I write as a clinician who has made a real effort to understand the fine-grained arguments of the theorist. I ask where that effort has led me.

In retrospect, it is clear that in fact I provided assistance to patients in the commission of suicide by counseling the withholding and/or the withdrawal of treatment, and by writing orders for such acts or omissions. Sometimes my actions fell easily into the category of not prolonging dying, but at other times, in hindsight, it now seems clear that my counseling and actions hastened or caused patients' deaths, that I helped patients bring their lives to an end. More disturbing, in retrospect, is the realization that too often my actions and advice crossed the line from objective counseling to paternalistic (or parentalistic) coercion. I find I have allowed my expert knowledge of patients' prudential interests—their very bleak prognoses and their present and future suffering—to discount their values, their desire to hang on to life, no matter how punishing. In the words of Prado and Taylor, my compassion moved me to act in ways contrary to patients' autonomy. This happened despite my considerable awareness and trepidation regarding the risk of patients falling victim to well-intentioned care providers who would impose their judgments upon care recipients.

Despite these negative judgments, I believe that my goals always were honorable. Compassion and empathy were my real strengths. I attempted to experience the feelings of patients as my own, and act as an extension of their will and need. I believe that the emotional experience of empathetic understanding, of emotional knowing, does yield real knowledge, as claimed by feminist writers. This knowledge can serve as the basis for decisions and action. In retrospect, I believe that my empathetic understanding of patients' dilemmas very often did legitimize my participation in decisions about withholding or withdrawing treatment—decisions having to do with hastening death to avoid intolerable suffering.

It seems to me that the principles of modern palliative care find their embodiment in the role played by the knowledgeable and empathetic caregiver. But is there a role for the detached observer who makes judgments based on facts alone, for whom compassion is essentially an extraneous and possibly troublesome emotion? Would a caregiver with that perspective be less of a threat to patient autonomy, be better able to assess objectively patients' values and interests, and act accordingly? In my reading for this essay I have been very impressed by the parallels between those holding the high ground of palliative care and the position of those who would favor increased availability of assisted suicide. Both are motivated to provide for patients an escape from the punishing last days of a terminal illness: palliative care by relief of physical symptoms and by addition of value/quality to the last days of living, and assisted suicide by offering the option of death when such a choice seems preferable to intractable suffering. Is it not possible that at the heart of the antipathy between advocates of palliative care and of assisted suicide there is a coincidence of goals?

With that thought in mind the question becomes what, if anything, might allow a physician to move with integrity across the ethical line so clearly drawn by Dr. Twycross. If I were to face again the terminal agony of my respected teacher, could I now inject potassium chloride into his vein to speed him to the end of his life? Although I am less sure, my answer is still probably no, but I do see in a fresh and clearer light three reasons why one might cross that line.

The first would be compassion, the capacity to really enter into the suffering of the terminally ill patient. The second would be an unequivocal understanding that the ending of the life would be preferable to the inescapable suffering being endured, that is, that death would be in the patient's best interests. The third is linked to the first: my humanity. Hume, in his *Enquiry*, lists *humane* as one of the epithets "known in all languages," and describes it as expressing "the highest merit which human nature is capable of attaining." In a later paragraph he writes, "that no qualities are more entitled to the good-will and approbation of mankind than benevolence and humanity."[14] Prado and Taylor, several times in their text, fall back on this word, without defining it; for example, "If theory and practice aren't reconciled regarding provision of assisted suicide, what is at risk is our humanity." Perhaps we are given to maintaining human life in hopeless circumstances because we have sanctified it, because we have actually qualified or curbed our own humanity for abstract ethical and/or religious reasons. More than once those observing patients suffering have commented to me: "You wouldn't treat a dog like that." Should my humanity permit me to cross the line to end intractable suffering?

Having acknowledged such a possibility, another question arises. How would knowingly hastening a patient's death affect *me*? More importantly, if assisted suicide and voluntary euthanasia were to become acceptable treatment options in the armamentarium of palliative care teams, what would this do to those caregivers who, individually and collectively, in the face of all the impersonal circumstances of modern scientific medicine, make such a difference to the last days of living for so many persons facing death?

Prado and Taylor say that when it comes to life and death decisions in the context of terminal illness and life-prolonging technology, we are "concept-poor"; that we are making the concept of suicide do too much work to cover quite disparate sorts of cases. They believe that we need finer-grained ways of describing what people do when they willingly succumb to delayed but inevitable death by requesting cessation of technological life support, and better ways to say what people do when they choose to relinquish lives that are in any case forfeit in anticipation of hopeless suffering. I agree.

The police called Dr. Morrison's action murder. When the judge dismissed that charge, the Crown called it manslaughter. The Attorney General wished for another classification, and for better guidelines. What kind of conceptual tools would help me wrestle more creatively with, and understand better, what I did when I injected opiate and anxiolytic into a desperate woman's vein to relieve her agony, and then, to my dismay, watched her pass in a few moments from suffering consciousness to death? What new conceptual apparatus would help me understand better my desperate desire to end quickly the physical and mental anguish of my esteemed teacher, and my equally strong desire not to cross the Twycross line?

It would appear that Dr. Morrison crossed the line of expectations of the ICU team; and when asked why, she did not have an answer. Prado and Taylor point out that the advent of life-prolonging technology has not changed the interpretation of the principle of beneficence, that is, of bringing about good. It is still taken to mean "keeping people alive"; and the principle of nonmaleficence, that is, of doing no harm, is assumed to mean "not letting people die," and certainly not killing them. But in the face of today's life-prolonging or too often death-

protracting technology, is it possible that the meaning of beneficence and nonmaleficence need to be reinterpreted; that in circumstances as extreme as those in which Morrison found
herself, beneficence might mean not only *not* preserving life,
but actively bringing it to an end; that when aiding or causing
death seems the only way to relieve extreme suffering, the principle of beneficence should override the appearance of maleficence? When, unintentionally, I hastened the death of the
desperately dyspneic woman, was I allowing beneficence to
override the appearance of maleficence? Was that what part of
me wanted to do for my anguished teacher? What held me
back? What failed to hold Morrison back?

I think such restraint had something to do with my fear of
the appearance of maleficence. Since Hippocrates, "do no
harm" has been one of medicine's sustaining principles. Con-
travention of that principle is one of the quickest ways to bring
upon oneself the opprobrium of clinical colleagues; and when
that happens, even unintentionally, it is extremely uncomfortable. Surely, that is what I feared most when the breathing of
the dyspneic woman before me grew slower and slower. On
the afternoon my teacher died, the nurse who was with me
was as distressed by his suffering as I was. But had I crossed
that imaginary line, had I acted in a way clearly designed to
relieve my teacher's suffering by ending his life, I think the
nurse's distress would have been even greater. But beyond her
distress, what would have been the effect of a life-ending act
by me on the team of caregivers of which she was a representative? Would it have undermined trust in me and shaken
faith in the rightness of the principles of palliative care?

In that crucible circumstance of my teacher's last hour,
did his best interests become secondary to those of the cause,
to the team's, to mine? Was this shift in priorities right? Ethical theorists have shed much light on what clinicians actually
do in the care of terminally ill patients. Is it possible, in the
light of these insights, for palliative care clinicians to move beyond the fear of appearances, to stay more humanely focused
on the reality of their patients' best interests? Can the theorists
help us to understand better those lines we fear to cross, and

to see more clearly the consequences of crossing those lines, both for ourselves and for those who need our care? I sincerely hope so.

1.   Suicide is most succinctly defined as intentionally caused self-destruction, and assisted suicide as self-killing with help. Tom Beauchamp's (1980) more refined definition holds that a person commits suicide if: 1) that person intentionally brings about his or her own death; 2) others do not coerce him or her to do the action; and 3) death is caused by conditions arranged by the person for the purpose of bringing about his or her own death.

Euthanasia, for the Greeks, meant a good or easy death. Its modern meaning is death caused by a surrogate acting in the best interests of a suffering patient. Voluntary euthanasia implies consent and awareness on the part of the patient.

The distinction between assisted suicide and voluntary euthanasia concerns the primacy of agency. If the patient is the primary agent, then it is assisted suicide; but if the clinician is the primary agent, it is voluntary euthanasia. The distinction is one of degree and perspective, and although there are very strong philosophical and legal arguments for making the distinction, in practice it is often blurred, and some experts think there is no important difference. For the purpose of this essay, assisted suicide and euthanasia are viewed as roughly equivalent.

2.   Hinton, 1967.

3.   Kübler-Ross, 1969.

4.   Hinton, 1967: 159.

5.   Du Boulay, 1984.

6.   Located in southeast London, it opened in 1967.

7.   Hospice and palliative care are terms used interchangeably, the latter preferred in Canada because of its more precise meaning in French translation.

8.   One of Dr. Saunders' famous aphorisms.

9.   "The Final Hours," *Maclean's*, March 9, 1998.

10.   Reported July 3, 1998, the *Kingston Whig-Standard*.

11.   Twycross, 1988: 2.

12.   Prado and Taylor, 1999.

13.   Prado and Taylor, 1999; criteria are slightly paraphrased.

14.   Hume, 1983: 17.

Jan Narveson

DEFINITIONS AND MORAL ISSUES

The Issue

Does assisted suicide differ from requested euthanasia? If
so, in what respects? First, in order to be able to discuss this
question, we need to differentiate what we mean by the terms
"assisted suicide" and "euthanasia." Only then we can proceed
to ask whether we should make legal or moral distinctions between assisted suicide and euthanasia: for example, making
the one permissible, the other not. If, after all, there were simply no difference between the two conceptually, then any
attempt to differentiate them legally or morally would be irrel-
evant and futile from the start.

Let us first address the relation between standard suicide
and assisted suicide. Prima facie, we can superficially determine that suicide is self-inflicted death, while assisted suicide
is death inflicted by someone else. In the special case that is of
interest here, assisted suicide is requested by the potential victim. This distinction is relevant because requesting assistance
in suicide is often regarded as tantamount to initiating it oneself. If I go to the bank to withdraw money from my account,
we say that "I withdrew it" rather than "the teller gave it to me
at my request," although the latter is what in fact happened.
(With automated bank machines, our "request" is punched
into a computer which then orders the machine to dispense

the requested amount. No one considers it a morally interesting distinction whether we withdraw our money from a sock, a machine or an account with a human intermediary.)

Is the involvement of such an intermediary relevant in matters of assisted suicide? Logically, we might answer with four possible replies: both suicide and assisted suicide are wrong; both are right; suicide is right while assisted suicide is wrong; or, assisted suicide is right and suicide wrong. For present purposes, I will eliminate two of these responses. I will assume that all readers will agree that suicide, while often ill advised and tragic, is nevertheless not to be morally condemned in the way that, for instance, murder is. The question hence becomes only whether the moral status of requested euthanasia is the same as (assisted) suicide. Do our reasons for thinking suicide to be outside moral condemnation transfer straight off to cases of assisted suicide?

When we describe someone's intervention in the death of another as "assisted suicide," we think of the assisting person as acting as an *agent* for the patient who invokes such aid. The role of this facilitator is logically akin to that of the bank teller who routinely facilitates a requested transaction. However, when we employ the terminology "requested euthanasia," we seek to characterize something quite different. We expect a request to be deliberately and thoroughly considered by the person whose action is being requested. We expect that this person addresses the moral significance of such a question independently. For example, if Jones is ill, and for reasons of his own sees his case as hopeless and wants to end his life, the recipient of this request must now decide whether Jones is indeed suffering to an extent that euthanasia should be contemplated. The requested agent who would facilitate the euthanasia must address her own conscience; she might conclude that euthanasia would be wrong in Jones' case, or even that euthanasia as such is immoral.

Can careful definition of our terms help to solve this problem? Here is a way of trying to do so. Suicide, as we have noted, is self-inflicted death. Assisted suicide should be compared to the taking of the lethal pill by the *patient*. He cannot, we'll suppose, take it himself, and so he requests someone else to put the pill in his mouth. On this analysis, assisted suicide amounts merely to other-applied suicide, or "suicide-at-a-distance," as it were. Hence, if suicide is permissible, we should also find assisted suicide permissible. Requested euthanasia, because it is requested by the patient, is fundamentally fulfilling the will of the *patient*. Suicide is motivated by a desire to eliminate suffering; it has the same end as euthanasia then: "easy death."

Humans are capable of addressing moral questions independently. Invoking the category of assisted suicide suggests that this point may be pushed to the side; talk of requested euthanasia moves the separate responsibility of the agent or facilitator toward the center. Which way are we to go?

A Parallel: The Epicurean Gambit

The ancient hedonist Epicurus proposed to settle once and for all the question of the immortality of the soul. Death, he said, is nothing to fear, for it is literally nothing: "Where we are, death is not; and where death is, we are not." So, why worry?

In response to Epicurus, some professing to accept his view go on to assert that nothingness is actually something rather alarming. Other, perhaps more sophisticated, thinkers assert that nothingness is not a special form of something: words like "nothing" and "nothingness" do not designate a unique and potentially frightening state of being, but instead indicate that there is not any being of the kind in question: such terms fail to designate at all, and so do not designate something strange or terrifying. Despite this, people appear to have a strong desire to continue to exist, to live. Death is the end of life as we know it, and because death is a state of affairs that fails to include ourselves, the rational person attempts to avoid death.

Was Epicurus correct in supposing that death is indeed the cessation of life as such? His contention amounts to an argument from definition. Death is the terminus of life, hence worries about what death will "be like" are unfounded because death won't be "like" *anything*.

On Definition

Might we quell our philosophical doubts by a stroke of the definitional pen? We should be suspicious of such maneuvers, for they may provide not the truth, but the appearance of truth. Truths-by-definition may represent, as Bertrand Russell once put it, the advantages of theft over honest toil. But in philosophy, unlike bank robbery, no real goods can be made off with in this way; for the truth is what we seek, and if what one has is false, it does not matter who else is fooled into thinking that we have what we want—for we don't.

The problem with Epicurus' argument can be highlighted through asking what the proponent of immortality is claiming. If we define "death" as "the end of life," then the astute immortalist can reformulate his own thesis. He can claim that, contrary to appearances, we do not in fact die; we are only misled into thinking that we die. Instead, he can insist on a necessary distinction between two meanings of the word "death." Death could be construed after Epicurus as absence of life—but it might also take on another meaning: what we mortals observe when we see people "dying" is what we may call the cessation of observable bodily activity. Modern neurological ideas and findings can lead us to refine this definition so that "bodily" is taken to include the nervous system. However, what Epicurus, the ancient Egyptians and many of the rest of us untutored folks observe is that people who used to be walking about, or at least breathing, cease to do any of that; further, the bodies that used to do so will naturally degenerate and decay.

To dust, in short, we return. And yet the immortalist insists that this does not settle the matter. Instead, the immortalist might argue that the soul, as an immaterial substance, has only a rough, extensional coexistence in relation to the body or nervous system. It might be argued that although the bodily system may cease to function, the soul continues to exist. This is a "dualist" response to the problem, and dualism is now almost universally rejected among savants. And it is certainly difficult to discuss meaningfully because of our inability to understand immaterial entities. Perhaps it will be possible, with subtle analysis, to dismiss dualism as meaningless, but if so, the analysis is going to have to be very subtle indeed: our acquaintance with our own thoughts, impressions, images and memories makes it notoriously difficult to analyze them as mere physical processes along with the nebula and the quantum phenomena and the rest. Dualism as a logical possibility does not die easily, even if we are hard put to understand it.

In any case, the immortalist might also build his case without recourse to dualism. If a particular soul is a configuration of material particles together with a certain set of psychological software, then why should it not be possible, at some point, for this body to be sufficiently reconstituted or reconfigured such that at some later time the person whose body it is resumes existence? Even if we suppose this takes millions of years and one wakes up on some other planet—well, what of it? For if the person in question has been as if in a sound sleep all that time, it will not seem to him as though any time has passed, despite the strangeness of his new surroundings. Psychological time is continuous, despite being a discontinuous, fractured subset of moments of physical time—like the movie, whose continuity to the viewer is generated from a highly discontinuous set of takes made over a period of perhaps several months.

If we can identify an item of some kind, we can also name it. The human capacity to define is apparently limitless. We define terms in a variety of ways—for example, by pointing, extracting meanings from contexts, drawing pictures or putting together combinations of sounds without sense (the slithey toves) or combinations whose parts are mutually incompatible (round squares). When successful, definitions allow the previously perplexed to identify that thing to which a term is intended to refer, or the properties it is intended to signify. But the name we give something cannot tell us what is actually going on in the world. We can name uninstantiated possibilities as well as actual ones, and we must have a look at the world itself, not just the language we use to talk about it, in order to find out what it's like.

Definition in Ethics

In moral philosophy, the repercussions of subtle mistakes expand enormously. There is a great deal of debate about method in moral theory—indeed there is debate regarding the very existence of moral theory, as a body of solid results arrived at by the incontrovertibly right method of addressing moral queries. Regardless, there is abundant discussion surrounding moral matters. Premises are identified, conclusions inferred and the result of this activity might be a real alteration of someone's previously held opinion, or perhaps the supplying of good grounds for an opinion on some matter about which no opinion was formerly held.

How are persuasive arguments constructed? Arguments extract conclusions from premises. They fail if their conclusions do not actually follow from these premises; and even if they do follow, they will fail to establish the acceptability of their conclusions if the premises from which they follow are not themselves true. Truth, of course, is what we desire; but arguments might also be considered successful if they are persuasive. An argument will not persuade if its premises are not accepted or if its conclusion does not seem to follow. It may, however, persuade when the premises are accepted and the conclusion does appear to follow, even if that conclusion differs considerably from what one had previously been inclined to think. This is why we want to argue from commonly accepted premises—"commonly" meaning here that they are common to the persuader as well as the persuadee, and not just the "community" or the average bystander. Common premises, especially in moral matters, are characteristically expressed in common language. Yet common language, as we have become acutely aware, can be ambiguous and vague. Either can lead to trouble.

A Notorious Example—Abortion and Defining "Life"

It may be instructive to employ an example from another problem area in applied ethics—the abortion issue. Discussions of abortion often arrive at a notorious impasse due to an alleged inability to define the term "human." There appears to be common agreement that killing *innocent people* is wrong. Who, however, are to be considered innocent people? If innocence is just a matter of not committing any crimes or any moral offenses that might deserve death, then embryos are innocent, as are trees. The question becomes whether embryos are among the entities whose lives are to be classified such that aborting them amounts to killing innocent *people*, which in turn amounts to murder. But where do we go from there?

At this point, many participants in this debate tell us that we have arrived at a fundamental question of definition—the definition of human life. Some will argue that human life begins at conception, therefore abortion is murder and should be commonly accepted as wrong. This makes abortion a classic case of a moral issue that turns on a point of definition.

It seems remarkable that this matter could seriously be claimed to reduce to a matter of definition. Definitions explain or clarify the meaning of words. Words are means of communication, and their definitions allow us to talk with one another. But that is all. In and of themselves, definitions prove nothing and so they can settle nothing. If several people in this discussion agree that murder is wrong—as they do—and yet deny that abortion is wrong, the most reasonable hypothesis regarding their position is that they do not think that fetuses and embryos are entities of the type such that they can be killed, *and* killing them is in the same moral category as killing adults or children. It may be argued, however, that the term "human" as it refers to embryos designates something different than "human" as applied in other contexts. The question becomes, what is it about these organisms which we refer to as human—the ones which we commonly agree it would be murder to kill—which makes it wrong to kill them? Then we may ask whether embryos have these properties in question.

And while this is an important question, it becomes readily apparent that it cannot be settled simply through definition.

The belief that definition has some kind of magic power to settle things on its own is a misperception; an illusion. Definitions are powerless in and of themselves. They are useful for communication and clarification, but that is all. Language is malleable and we often manipulate and redefine our terms in order to suit particular needs.

In the case of abortion, it is clear that the frequently employed word "human" is ambiguous. It is also vague. Human organisms develop continuously over a long period, from conception to full maturity. It is very difficult, if not impossible, to nonarbitrarily isolate where, upon this continuum, human organisms become the kind of entities that have the "right to life." This is the crux of so-called "slippery slope" arguments. Words are often vague, and yet we sometimes require precise definitions to bring clarity to our discussions. Definition is always subordinate to the primary purpose of communication.

Participants in disagreements about abortion should recognize that their concern actually hinges on a moral, and not a linguistic, matter. "Conservatives" in the abortion matter insist that what makes it wrong to kill people is their membership in a certain biological species, homo sapiens, and that embryos are indeed organisms of that species. Others hold that embryos are not yet the kind of beings that qualify for a genuine right to life, following from a narrower understanding of what it means to be "human." Both parties need to get into substantive moral theory to explain why their particular choice is the one to go by in awarding rights to life. Definition alone won't do that work for them.

Likewise, the mere definition of the word "death" cannot reveal whether and why the condition so designated is a bad thing. However, attempts to clarify and reach consensus on a definition of death might well elucidate the reasons why we think it important to avoid death—or why some individuals, in certain circumstances, might seek death. Attempts to know and understand what death involves constitute a very different kind of inquiry from questions of whether it is to be considered "good" or "bad."

Three Types of Definition

The preceding remarks about definition may require qualification, for thus far I have been assuming that definition reflects one of two basic types: "Reportive" and "Stipulative."

The "Reportive" definition tells us of a word's current usage among a relevant linguistic group. Such a definition will be accurate or not insofar as it correctly tracks and predicts the linguistic behavior of typical speakers in that group.

The "Stipulative" definition does not report preexisting usage, but formulates a possible usage. In principle, we could attach any meaning to any word by this means, which might cause one to ask the point of such definitions. One response is that we can use stipulative definitions for clarification. Through usage we are able to make our terms artificially precise. For example, if we define "tall" as "at least six feet high," we make the term artificially precise, relative to preexisting usage, but we don't lose track of it altogether. On the other hand, when a new scientific term such as "quark" is introduced, it has no precedent (which is appropriate in that case, because quarks were newly discovered entities, so why not coin a brand-new word for them).

But there is a third kind of definition: "Theoretical" definition, also known as "Scientific" definition. Such definitions move beyond the strictly linguistic; they purport to be what used to be known as "Real" definitions. For example, when we define "water" as "H_2O," clearly, "H_2O" is no part of the *meaning* of the term "water" as used by ordinary people who have never heard of chemical theory. Yet, all that stuff which we do call "water" in ordinary meaning is in fact H_2O, or so we are told by scientists. Assuming, as we will, that they know what they're talking about, we could state as a *fact* that "Water is water"! That is, "water" in the familiar sense as defined by ostension and general contact with it, is also water in the sense of H_2O. In the lab, no doubt, the word "water" would often

37

have a stipulated sense: instead of meaning "that stuff," it *means* "H_2O." But what makes this stipulated definition an applicable one regarding the familiar use of the term is the universal extensional correspondence: the familiar stuff is in fact a compound of hydrogen and oxygen.

The Theoretical term "definition" might be objected to, since these formulae are not designated to explicate meanings, as such, but to explain the way things are. The objection is answered, however, by the point just made: theoretical definitions often do tell us the essence of the things designated by the term—the definition tells us what makes them, scientifically speaking, what they are.

It is not always easy to apply these distinctions to given proposals, but there is a useful application to our present subject of death and its procurement: the term "brain dead." This term does bear a stipulative definition, indicating brains that have ceased to function. Such a brain can be said to have *died* in a sense closely analogous to that in which we die—it stops doing what it normally does, and if it stops for long, it stops permanently. But the definition is by no means merely stipulative. The term "brain dead" is also instructive in providing a better physiological specification of human death. The idea is that brain-dead people, though their bodily organs may continue to function, *might as well* be dead simpliciter: to the best of our knowledge, brain death permanently terminates the consciousness of its sufferer. Insofar as this is so, brain death *is* death, so far as we are concerned. Hence, the notion of brain death formulates a good theoretical definition of death. The cessation of brain function largely gives way to cessation of primary nervous-system activity.

A Caution

Let us now move to the issue of abortion. An analogous theoretical attempt to define "human" along the lines, say, of genetic profile, would not have the efficacy of the brain-death analysis of death. Reference to the *homo sapiens* genome will not resolve the abortion controversy, because many things (zygotes, embryos, fetuses, brain-dead ex-persons) clearly do have the human genome, yet they lack other important qualities designated by familiar uses of words like "human" or "person." A theoretical definition will not aid in resolving a moral or humanistic dispute unless it provides relevant insight into the subject as seen by *all parties* to the dispute. No one disputes that human beings die, in our observational sense of the term. The concept of brain death helpfully pins down the central feature of our bodies that accounts for death in that usual sense of the term. But proponents of liberal abortion do not agree that the presence of human genes is all it takes to be entitled to the right to life. In their view, more is needed.

It becomes apparent that theoretical definitions, while extremely important in many contexts, do not resolve all problems by themselves. As always, clarification of the usage of the defined term *ex ante* is required; but when provided, our problem may not be solved.

Consider once again the question of immortality. The experience of humankind, carefully sifted, actually supports the Epicurean conclusion, if any. But neither scientific data nor abstract definitions sufficiently prove that there is no life after death. Careful consideration of the options is required: Do after-life hypotheses really make sense? What could possibly constitute evidence for or against them? Insofar as relevant "evidence" requires facts that humans can know while we are alive, then we lack evidence for such hypotheses. Tales of voices from the beyond are insufficient on several levels; what we know of physics and other relevant sciences provides no scope for nonbodily residence; and so on. But it is such things we need before we can definitively reject the Epicurean view. And, of course, there remains the logical possibility that no evidence *is* available to us, and yet once we die we acquire the sort of direct experience that would confirm postmortem life. At present, we may say that immortality is an *unreasonable* hypothesis, yes—but not a definitively refuted one. Definitions may help to clarify the issue; but they cannot resolve it for us.

Redefining the Issue: Requested Euthanasia or Assisted Suicide?

The case of a patient who wants someone else to administer a procedure terminating his life, because he is unable to facilitate this procedure for himself, appears to correspond to either the description of requested euthanasia or assisted suicide. The patient does ask for the termination of his life—the act is *requested*; however, any person who facilitates this termination will have assisted the patient in his request—the act is *assisted*. But should this event be conceived as suicide or euthanasia? The agent may be described as having *committed suicide* if the provider of that service is viewed as simply a means, an instrumental link between the patient's will and his demise. But the provider might also be perceived as having performed euthanasia, assuming that the patient was indeed seeking the cessation of what he came to see as an intolerable life.

Can we assume that the patient was indeed seeking the cessation of what he perceived as an intolerable life? We will assume that we do have adequate reason to think that this is what he believes. But what are we to say of the hoped-for assistant? Since he is a fellow human, intentionally performing an optional action, it cannot be literally true that he is simply an instrument in a chain from the act of the patient's will to the patient's desired death. However, the assistant might alternately take the decided view that this is exactly how he should perceive his role in the situation. He may believe that he *owes* it to his suffering fellow person to help him out of his misery by acting in accord with the patient's wishes and by refraining to inject his own opinions into the equation.

In the movie *Stalingrad*, there is a heart-wrenching scene in which severely wounded soldiers lie in the snow as their retreating comrades tramp by. One of them cries out, to anyone who will listen, "Shoot me, shoot me!" A member of the passing army could hardly doubt the sincerity of the soldier's request, and most would likely find it not only sincere but also reasonable. And yet no one is portrayed as providing the requested assistance—though we may well feel that close friends of the wounded man might have responded different-ly. Regardless, what cannot be denied is that persons subject-ed to such requests have a real decision to make. Are they merely assisting their fellow men in doing what the latter can-not do themselves? Or are they making a moral decision that this man's life is truly not worth living beyond the present point?

Consider the following situation. Suppose that soldier Gerd believes that people in the condition of the wounded man, Hans, should persevere and cling to life, however pain-ful, for as long as possible. And yet suppose Gerd *also* believes that Hans has a right to decide for himself the question of how long one should endure life. Moreover, Gerd believes that if Hans' response to the dilemma were different from Gerd's own, nevertheless he has no business ignoring Hans' request when it is, after all, Hans' life at stake. So Gerd believes that the thing to do is offer his assistance if that is what Hans really wants. Yet isn't Gerd's original intuition defensible too?

If we translate the scene to a modern hospital, the patient lying in bed, his body swathed in bandages, his arms stuck with needles, his life a maze of medical paraphernalia and his consciousness a painful or dopey daze, we face the same issue. Whatever we conclude, it is not an issue that can be resolved merely by attending very carefully to the meaning of the phrases "assisted suicide" and "requested euthanasia."

We might imagine a future time when the public attitude toward this subject has altered, and it is generally felt that people should decide for themselves whether they wish to die, with others allowed to assist them in this request, if they are inclined to do so. We can further imagine that such a service might become generally available, such that one could look in the telephone book for providers of that kind of assistance, when required. In such circumstances, it is easy to believe that such assistants could perceive themselves as morally impar-tial, and as simply providing a link in the chain from a deci-sion to action that cannot be completed by its requester. In such a circumstance, the phrase "assisted suicide" would be the natural linguistic choice. Regardless, the moral issue endures. And insofar as it is thought not to, it won't be newly clarified definitions, but new attitudes, that settle it.

Conclusion

Definition is an attempt to make terms clear. Definitions can remind us what we have overlooked in the course of inquiry or argument. They can also focus on aspects that, having been brought to attention, might be further investigated and developed. And sometimes, definitions can link previously unrecognized aspects of the debate with already established considerations or with the results of new scientific research. In all of these cases, moral judgments may be enhanced; but in none of them do the definitions by themselves suffice to establish or refute a moral claim. In the case of assisted suicide versus euthanasia, the factor of request is common to both terms; however, the term "assisted suicide" downplays the responsibility of the assistant, while "requested euthanasia" emphasizes that person's role. Which term we choose to employ requires and reflects a moral judgment that will involve much more than simply understanding definitions more precisely.

C. G. Prado

AMBIGUITY AND SYNERGISM IN "ASSISTED SUICIDE"

Present debate about "managed death"[1] is vitiated by ambiguity. Various forms of managed death—not delaying or hastening death in terminal illness—are being lumped together as "assisted suicide." But the bulk of managed death is not help in *self*-destruction; rather it is compassionate causing of terminal patients' deaths by physicians complying with those patients' desire to end their suffering. Ambiguity poses a worrisome issue because we are beginning to acknowledge what has long gone on in our hospitals, to more openly accept so-called "assisted suicide" and inclining to legalize its provision. We need to frame sound policies to govern the practice if it is legalized. We cannot afford to let debate, legislation and regulative policy be jeopardized by unreflective acceptance and equivocal description of different kinds of managed death as all cases of self-destruction.

Still, misconception and misrepresentation of managed death as assisted suicide are neither accidental nor simply mistaken. What prompts both is a combination of circumstantial, moral and legal pressures that provide some warrant for thinking of managed death primarily in terms of patients' self-determination. Terminal patients who choose to die, rather than endure pointless pain and degradation, cannot readily enact their decisions by themselves and need the help of others, usually physicians, to achieve their ends—in both senses of the phrase. Because terminal patients' circumstances both prompt desires to not delay or hasten death and dictate that others help enact their decisions, the historically new term "assisted suicide" emphasizes the role of patients' decisions and de-emphasizes the role of others' actions to construe and describe managed death as essentially *suicide*, even if in fact caused by others. Additionally, as is pointed out in the Canadian Senate's report on assisted suicide and euthanasia, use of pivotal terms in the managed-death debate is "seldom based on...literal meaning." Instead, terms are used in ways that reflect and promote "a specific moral or ethical perspective."[2] A crucial aspect of this usage and the thinking it reflects is limitation of responsibility. Emphasizing patients' own decisions, in order to construe managed death as assisted suicide, attributes primary responsibility for managed death to patients. If physicians managing patients' deaths are assisting *suicide*, their moral and legal responsibilities are more narrowly defined and may be more leniently assessed than if they are performing euthanasia. If patients' decisions are given definitive priority over physicians' death-causing actions, the latter are cast as those of agents carrying out patients' decisions and not those of individuals acting in their own stead.

* * *

Webster's Unabridged[3] dictionary defines suicide as "the intentional taking of one's own life." Suicide is *self*-killing. Causing another's death for compassionate reasons is euthanasia. In managed death, physicians typically cause patients' deaths directly or indirectly, so it would seem that managed death is not assisted suicide. Unfortunately, matters cannot be settled by recourse to the dictionary. Jan Narveson rightly points out that "it is not possible to separate neatly questions of definition from questions of moral substance."[4]

The substantial question about managed death is whether it is morally permissible for terminally ill individuals to take their own lives and for others to help them do so or to take those individuals' lives at their behest. The basic issue is whether "life is the possession of the person who lives it" or is "a gift, of which we are custodians with certain duties."[5] Proponents of managed death, who hold the former view, think disposition of one's own life is covered by personal autonomy, so they think managed death is morally permissible in the right circumstances. They also think that assistance should be provided where those wishing to end their lives for good reason are unable to do so unaided. Because proponents of managed death emphasize personal autonomy, they are comfortable with describing it as assisted suicide, since that description puts the emphasis where they think it belongs: on patients' own choices to forfeit time left to them in order to avoid suffering and debasement.

Opponents of managed death think life is an unrenounceable gift and see managed death as impermissible killing, regardless of who bears primary responsibility for causing death, how insistent the demands of those wishing to die or how compassionate the motives of those assisting self-destruction or causing death on request. Because opponents emphasize the causing of death, they focus on physicians' actions in managed death and see it as euthanasia. Additionally, they think patients' decisions to forfeit life are always suspect, due to the effects of depression and coercive influences. These include such things as physicians seeking closure when treatment proves ineffective, families being unable to bear the burdens of lengthy terminal illness and institutions acting to reduce the cost of health care.

What complicates matters considerably is that physicians do not just *help* in suicide, as does Strato, for instance, when he holds a sword for Brutus to fall on in the last act of *Julius Caesar*. Nor do physicians only perform euthanasia when patients want to die but cannot manage suicide on their own. Physicians sometimes do both, but there is a *synergism*[6] involved in some cases of managed death that needs to be better understood. Sheryl Gay Stolberg captures the key point in outlining a task force's production of guidelines for Oregon's recent Death With Dignity Act. Stolberg remarks that in the guidelines

> [e]ach word is carefully chosen, most notably the phrase "physician-assisted suicide." The term is not used in the Oregon Death

With Dignity Act; proponents prefer the phrase "hastened death" while opponents favor "euthanasia." But the task force settled on "physician-assisted suicide"...because the phrase is commonly accepted in the bioethics literature, *and because it correctly implies participation by both the patient and the doctor.*[7]

Understanding some cases of managed death as assisted suicide on the strength of patients' and physicians' joint involvement means that managed death is *suicide* because of the primacy of patients' decisions, and is *assisted* suicide because of the practical necessity of physicians' involvement.

There are several ways to conceive of how patients and physicians participate in managing death. First, physicians hastening or not delaying terminal patients' deaths may be merely a matter of them acting in patients' stead. From this "agent" perspective, managed death is assisted suicide because physicians only do for patients what is impractical or impossible for patients to do themselves. Second, physicians hastening or not delaying death may be performing requested or voluntary euthanasia, acting in their own stead for compassionate reasons though responding to patient requests. From this euthanatic perspective, description of managed death as assisted suicide is at best seriously misleading. Third, it may be that patients and physicians both act for ill-understood reasons, which include the effects of depression, circumstantial influences, professional limitations, financial considerations and problematic beliefs and values. From this critical perspective, phrases like "managed death" and "assisted suicide" are euphemisms for diverse actions ultimately driven by professional, emotional and/or economic expediency. This is, again, a denial that managed death is assisted suicide. Fourth, it could be that patients and physicians act jointly to achieve what they believe is the best resolution of a hopeless and punishing situation. From this synergistic perspective managed death may be neither suicide nor euthanasia; instead it may be something new, prompted by medicine's recently acquired capacities. The phrase "assisted suicide" may be a term of art still in the process of being defined.

The first thing needing to be done is to sort out what can be literally described as assisted suicide. While we can extend the meaning of the word "suicide" to accommodate the situations generated by modern medicine's new ability to protract death, we cannot eradicate the difference between *oneself* causing one's own death and *another* causing one's death. The concept of self-destruction may accommodate the agent and/or synergistic senses of hastening or not delaying of death, but there is need to consider the extent to which others' actions are tolerated before application of the concept of suicide is compromised or requires clarification. The difficulty is that the concept of suicide as "the intentional taking of *one's own* life" is silent on assistance. Tom L. Beauchamp offers criteria for suicide that are doubly useful here. First, the criteria differentiate suicide proper from other forms of death by requiring that suicide be *intentional* and *uncoerced*, and that death be *"caused by conditions arranged by the person for the purpose of bringing about his or her own death."*[8] Second, while Beauchamp's third criterion is intended to exclude coincidental causes of death, it opens the door to others' uncoercive assistance in suicide because some solicited actions by others may qualify as "conditions arranged by the person." This allows for someone else's actions to be part of what a suicidist sets in motion in taking his or her life, so those actions, even though the actions of another, may not compromise suicide as self-destruction.

There are two different ways of assisting suicide that preserve the primary agency required by Beauchamp's criteria and the concept of self-destruction. Suicide may be *facilitated* in that the means to end life are provided. For example, a physician may assist suicide by providing a lethal prescription that a patient can use or not use without the physician's further involvement. In facilitated suicide it is up to the potential suicidist whether or not to employ the means provided, and it is the suicidist's own act which causes death.[9] Suicide also may be *enabled* in that there is preparation of a lethal device needing only to be activated. For example, a physician may assist suicide by setting up an intravenous drip into which potassium chloride is introduced by activating a controlling device. In enabled suicide the suicidist's role is minimal and the apparatus provided is adapted to her or his specific situation, but it is still the suicidist who activates the apparatus. What is central here is that in both facilitated and enabled suicide, individuals' decisions are enacted by those individuals themselves.

Difficulties in distinguishing assisted suicide from euthanasia begin with enabled suicide when enablement shades off into what initially looks to be euthanatic action on others' parts. Consider two cases. In one a patient is so debile that he or she needs help in activating whatever suicide-enabling device has been provided.[10] In such cases the patient may be able to do no more than whisper "Do it now," yet we would likely consider that utterance in effect an act of self-destruction. In another, a patient is capable of activating the device but prefers that someone else activate it.[11] The patient's reluctance may be due to concern for others. For instance, the patient may want to spare a devoutly religious partner the burdensome knowledge that he or she committed suicide. In these cases, assistance goes beyond enablement of self-destruction, but still seems not to make a material difference to the suicidal nature of the resulting death, so it seems that the participation of physicians in causing death may be tolerated by the concept of suicide. This looks most plausible if we take as the paradigm hastening or not delaying the deaths of patients whose lives are being technologically sustained and whose capacity for independent action is seriously limited. In these cases it does appear that patients' expressed decisions essentially constitute acts of self-destruction, even if the mechanics of causing death are left to physicians. It is these cases that generate the apparent need for and possibility of the agent and synergistic senses of assistance in suicide.

Whether or not with reference to Beauchamp's third criterion, managed death is understood as assisted suicide by construing patients' expression of their desire to die as patients' establishing conditions for the purpose of bringing about their own deaths. The trouble with this interpretation is that it construes managed death as assisted suicide solely in the agent sense, and by casting physicians as mere agents, it un-derestimates their role and influence and reduces their moral responsibility for causing death. To better understand proper attribution of responsibility we can distinguish different de-grees by considering several locutions. In the case of *suicide*, the suicidist is able to say, truly and before the fact, "*I* will cause my death." *Per impossible* the suicidist would be able to say, truly and after the fact, "*I* caused my death." In the case of euthanasia, whether or not requested, a person other than the dying individual is able to say, truly and before the fact, "*I* will cause *his/her* death," and truly and after the fact, "I caused *her/his* death." In the case of assisted suicide in the agent sense, physicians act in compliance with patients' instruc-tions. Supposedly this is assistance in suicide where physi-cians' actions are merely conditions established by patients for the purpose of bringing about their own deaths. Patients then could say, truly and before the fact, "*I* will cause my death by having *him/her* kill me," and physicians would say, truly and before the fact, "*I* will cause *her/his* death" and, truly and after the fact, "*I* caused *her/his* death."

Appropriate physicians' locutions in assisted suicide in the (putative) "agent" sense are the same as are appropriate to eu-thanasia, which raises the question of whether one person can act merely as an agent for another when the action in question is one with important moral significance. It seems decisive for a negative answer that the reasons physicians would comply with patients' requests to cause patients' deaths are the same reasons they might perform euthanasia. This brings out that however obedient to patient requests, physicians would have their own reasons to cause death and so would be acting in their own moral stead despite their compliance. It is incon-ceivable that morally responsible physicians would cause pa-tients' deaths just because they were asked to do so. At best, then, assisted suicide in the "agent" sense is a complex action where patients may be said to commit suicide according to Beauchamp's third criterion, but physicians may be said to perform (requested) euthanasia. The "agent" sense of assisted suicide is at best problematic. Understanding managed death as assisted suicide on the basis of physicians' actions being no more than conditions established by patients for causing their own deaths is an unacceptable gloss on complex participation by physicians and patients. The complexity in question is indicated by the locutions appropriate to the synergistic causing of death: what is necessary is that patients choosing to die, and assisting physicians, be able to say, truly and before the fact, "*We* will cause this death," and that physicians be able to say, truly and after the fact, "*We* caused his/her death."[12] These "We..." locutions attribute shared responsibility for death, thereby showing physicians' actions to be more than their merely acting in compliance with patients' requests, and patients' requests to be more than simply initiating a causal chain with fatal results.

What emerges here is that the ambiguity of the managed death debate is worse than one over assisted suicide and euthanasia. Proponents and opponents of managed death may be arguing over the permissibility of "assisted suicide" *either* in the agent or synergistic senses of assistance in self-destruction, and contrasting or identifying each of these with euthanasia.

* * *

So far we have a sort of hierarchy, with *un*assisted suicide as the base of an inverted pyramid of levels of increasing involvement by others. Going from no involvement by others to the next level up we have such cases as Strato holding Brutus' sword. The cases do not concern us because physicians would not help patients commit suicide in this way. Strato was a servant, nearly a slave, and had to follow Brutus' orders in a manner no physician would or could do. The next step up in level of involvement is assistance in self-destruction in the *facilitated* suicide sense, that is, where the means for self-destruction are provided but the suicidist acts alone. Next is *enabled* suicide, where the means for self-destruction are provided in a quite particular way suited to the potential suicidist's circumstances, requiring minimal activation by the potential suicidist, and most likely involving time-constraints. Supposedly, the next step up would be to assisted suicide in the *agent* sense. The idea here is that another acts to cause death at the suicidist's order. In these cases the other's actions supposedly are conditions established by the suicidist to cause his or her death. In theory, the other's actions are comparable to the mechanical behavior of some death-causing device, but this is vitiated by the fact that all competent, responsible persons are moral agents in their own right. This means that they cannot do something immoral simply because ordered to do so.[13] Physicians assisting suicide would, of course, be competent, responsible people, hence not able to take patients' lives simply because asked to by patients. The point is that no one person can act purely as another person's *instrument* where the actions done have moral significance. The "agent" sense of assisted suicide is without content. Hypnotized or incompetent individuals or slaves might perform acts serving as others' instrument, but physicians managing patients' deaths are decidedly not in that group.

The vacuity of the "agent" sense of assisted suicide prompts the next move up in others' involvement, which is to assisted suicide in the *synergistic* sense. Here we supposedly have two individuals acting as one, in that the actions of the physician assisting suicide complete and enact the decision made by the patient wishing to hasten or not delay his or her death. The trouble here is that however disposed we might be to accept the viability of the synergistic sense, and to understand many or most cases of managed death in its terms, we need to deal with the fact that physicians have fiduciary responsibilities regarding their patients' well-being. Those responsibilities do not permit hastening or delaying death merely to comply with patients' expressed desires. Morality, legality and professional ethics will not allow death on demand. The "*We* will cause/caused death" locutions do not just attribute responsibility equally; they carry normative weight. That is, their proper applicability requires that physicians' actions complete patients' decisions in the sense that physicians agree with those decisions and see the consequent actions as in patients' best interests. Physicians may find themselves in a position where they must respect patients' suicidal decisions, when patients refuse life-sustaining treatment, but then they would not be *assisting* suicide. In such cases they would simply be unable to contravene patients' decisions and do what they themselves thought best.

* * *

It is necessary to appreciate the synergistic nature of physicians' roles in managed death in order to make out the best case for managed death being assisted suicide. That is, it is the synergistic nature of patients' and physicians' cooperation that makes it possible to consider deaths actually caused by physicians' actions instances of patients' suicides. However, what is central is not just patients' expressed desires and physicians' willing compliance, but physicians' *discernment of patients' intentions*. Normally, people's intentions are evident in what they *do*; in managed death the whole point is that their physicians effect patients' intentions. The problem that arises, given patients' and physicians' respective circumstances, is that physicians, aware of patients' conditions, prospects and suffering, too readily may construe patients' despairing expressions as entailing suicidal intentions. In particular, they may construe patients' expressed desire for death as suicidal intention. Physicians then may see themselves as effecting the intentions of patients when they are in fact initiating death-hastening or non-delaying action. In short, physicians may be predisposed to take too much for granted on the basis of bleak prognoses and evident distress, and start to see suicidal intention where there is only despondent recognition that life is all but over.

The issue here is the difference between desire and intention, and the fact that because of the difference, it is likely that Beauchamp's criteria are not met in many if not most cases of managed death. If so, "suicide" is inapplicable in those cases, and provision of euthanasia is passing as assistance in self-destruction.

The majority of terminal patients are helped to die in ways running from passive methods, such as not treating pneumonia with antibiotics, to active methods, such as removing ventilators, to more intrusive methods, such as administering too much morphine. Patients usually play no causal role in their deaths beyond asking for help in dying, expressing a desire to not have their deaths protracted or simply asserting their wish that death relieve them of their suffering. Managed death nonetheless is thought of as essentially suicide, whether or not the phrase "assisted suicide" is used, because patients' desire not to live on in the circumstances they find themselves is taken as decisive, and causing death by whatever means is deemed to be only enacting patients' own self-destructive decisions. Typically, the operant idea is that physicians act as patients' agents in the sense rejected above, but there may be more synergistic understandings of physicians' role. However, other problems aside, this understanding of managed death works only if patients' desires and intentions coincide. The trouble is that while desires and intentions may not coincide, their not coinciding is a possibility that many physicians neglect or contest. For instance, Arthur Caplan finds it "hard...to imagine a sincere desire to die without the intent."[14] Caplan is a physician who has reflected seriously on managed death and contributed extensively to its debate. If he fails to see a significant difference between a sincere *desire* to die and the *intention* to die, we can be sure that many of his peers share his view.

A thought-experiment will prove useful to make the point. Imagine that we could *will* ourselves to die, that we could stop our hearts by an act of will just as we can tense a muscle. Assisted suicide would be unnecessary and the concept probably unformed, and there would never be need to fathom individuals' intentions regarding their own deaths.[15] If we imagine we could will our deaths, it becomes clear that we might *want* to die but still not will our deaths. It is possible to have even a very strong desire and not form the corresponding intention, to not resolve to realize the desire. If we had the ability to will our deaths—that is, to enact our intentions by sheer thought—some might want to die but lack the courage to end their lives either by an act of will, an overt act or a request to someone else. Individuals could desperately want suffering to end but be profoundly fearful of personal annihilation. Again, deeply religious people enduring anguish could pray for death but not form the intention to die because forming that intention would be an unpardonable sin. A person can want something very much without intending to do or get it or even to arrange that it be done or gotten for him or her. This means suicidal intention may be absent from the most genuine desire for death. The import of this is that physicians cannot accept expressions of a desire for death as reflecting resolved intentions to die. This much may be obvious, and certainly physicians asked to cease or not initiate life-sustaining treatment are careful to assess patients' sincerity and competence. However, the difference between desire and intention makes possible that patients' expressed desire for death, and even requests for help in dying, may be only heartfelt pleas *that someone else cause their deaths*. It is perfectly possible for patients to *want* to die, to *not* form the intention to die, either by their action or by requesting physicians to cause death, *and* to long for physicians to cause death.

Patients might very much want to die without intending either to kill themselves or to arrange that they be killed, because they are unwilling to bear the responsibility for their own deaths. However longed-for and welcome death might be, patients might simply not be prepared to cause it directly or indirectly by asking it be done by another. But those same patients may sorely wish that those caring for them will end their lives. Heartfelt expressions like "Let it end!" may be avowals of the intent to die, or they may be prayers, or they may be pleas to physicians to put a stop to pain. What such expressions may be designed to do is to prompt physicians to propose cessation or noninitiation of treatment or to take more direct death-causing measures. This attempt to shift the responsibility for death onto physicians is what Elizabeth Kristol describes as patients availing themselves of a "soothing moral shroud."[16] Patients who are desperate but either irresolute about ending their lives or unwilling to take responsibility for doing so may look to their physicians to take matters in hand. Physicians are, after all, experts we "entrust with a wide range of decisions regarding our well-being."[17] If *they* take on the hastening or not delaying of death, they provide "an escape from the burden of autonomous choice" and, of course, from the responsibility for ending life. The irony here is that if physicians routinely interpret patients' expressed desires to die as requests for assistance in suicide, they nullify many patients' determination not to be responsible for their own deaths, thereby heedlessly shifting back onto vulnerable patients the responsibility for death, which they do not want to bear and are trying to evade.

Mistaking expressions of desire for expressions of intention is contextually justified to some extent in medical contexts. Most hospitalized terminal patients are at least practically unable to take their own lives, and some are physically unable to do so. The only option open to many with respect to bringing about their own deaths is to starve themselves, but that is a hard way to die and requires as well cooperative noninterference for a fairly considerable period of time. The result is some warrant to take expressions of desire for death as tantamount to expressions of intent to die and/or requests for help in self-destruction. The fact is that expressing their desires is all many patients can do to realize their intended objectives. Unfortunately, the warrant regularly is pushed too far for reasons having less to do with patients' incapacities than with impracticality, unreflective compassion, and professional and institutional considerations. Most patients are capable of taking some pills or activating suicide-enabling apparatus. Providing hospitalized patients with suicide-facilitating doses of drugs is acceptable enough, so facilitated suicide is feasible. Enabled suicide is much less so. Rigging up suicide-enabling devices for patients is not only impractical, it appears senseless to physicians who can themselves easily cease to protract or hasten patients' deaths. In addition, facilitating or enabling suicide also appears inhumane to physicians who can save patients the trauma of taking their own lives. Moreover, some physicians see provision of help in dying as a medical procedure, hence something they should administer, not something patients need do for themselves.

These factors not only render patient incapacity a secondary obstacle to facilitated or enabled suicide, they incline physicians to risky liberality in reading patients' intentions. It is then a small step to second-guessing or anticipating patients' intentions in light of expert opinion about what is in patients' best interests. The trouble is that if someone who is dependent on others expresses a wish, and is perceived as unable to do more than that to attain the thing wished for, the expression of desire is likely to be taken as a kind of imperative. But this tendency violates personal autonomy to the extent that intentions are imposed where there may be only desires.

* * *

The pivotal nature of the desire/intention difference not only requires that physicians correctly discern patients' intentions, it raises questions about how those intentions are formed. Suicide not only must be intentional, it must be a rational act in the sense of being autonomously and intentionally done for good reason. If suicide is not rational, there may be little we can do about it in some cases, but certainly providing assistance in its commission cannot be justified. To be rational, suicide must be soundly deliberated, cogently motivated, prescribed by well-grounded values and in the agent's best interests.[18] Assistance cannot be given if these requirements are not met because it would be compounding a wrong morally, legally and professionally.[19] The trouble is that terminal illness makes the rationality of suicide problematic. It impairs reasoning, skews motivation, distorts values and obscures interests. Terminal illness also makes patients vulnerable to undue influence and promotes abrogation of responsibility. Worry about the cost of treatment, shame of dependency, a physician's evident expectation, a partner's or a relation's unintentionally oppressive sympathy, any or all of these may combine with depression to confuse patients and make them too receptive to real or imagined suggestions. There is a real danger that willingness to help someone end his or her life could subtly compel that person to accept help in dying or relieve her or him of autonomous choice in the way Kristol describes.

* * *

Given the nature of terminal illness, a great deal of what is done once treatment is initiated is construed by physicians as helping someone to die. This is what managing death is all about; treatment of terminal illness cannot aim at *curing* anyone, so treatment is basically an easing and protraction of death. The importance of this is that to attending physicians, determining when patients might be allowed to die is something done in the context of the overall caring for those patients. From this wider perspective, actually causing or ceasing to protract death looks to be an integral part of medical care, and it looks as if too much is being made by philosophers and lawyers of particular actions like stopping administration of antibiotics, shutting off a ventilator or even administering a lethal dose of some medication. From this point of view, patients' intentions regarding death decrease in importance because their options involve only small temporal differences. Additionally, while a good deal can be done to make dying easier without hastening death, a good deal can be done to hasten death without either directly causing it or just letting the underlying illness run its course. If physicians see caring for the terminally ill as including death management, it can appear that a particular death-hastening treatment-decision and action are simply part of a complex process and not ones calling for special debate. Still, even if much of this is acceptable, what is harder to see is how causing death in helping someone through the process of dying comes to be assisting *suicide*.

The real problem is that we are concept-poor regarding recent developments in medical treatment of terminal patients. We have acquired the capacity to protract death faster than we have learned to conceptualize the actions necessary to end that protraction. As suggested, there is a synergistic character to the participation of physicians and patients in hastening or not delaying death in terminal illness. The phrase "assisted suicide" is being used in the contemporary euphemistic manner to denote this synergistic ending of death's protraction, but while ending death's protraction is ending life, it is not suicide. Managing death is something new generated by two main conditions: that life is being artificially sustained[20] and that life can be sustained well past the point at which survival is of benefit. These conditions have made it necessary to make decisions about when to no longer delay death. In doing so, the conditions have made it possible to hasten death. This is because good arguments for ceasing to delay death, for example, because of pointless suffering, are good arguments for hastening death where it would otherwise be too long in coming. Many have adopted the view that not delaying death is morally and legally permissible; many others concur and believe that hastening death is morally permissible and should be legally permissible. Death management, which includes hastening and not delaying death, is thought of as assisted suicide and often called that because of the centrality of patients' expressed preparedness to die when it is possible for them to continue living, though under unacceptable conditions.

But death management, however in accord with patients' wishes for or acceptance of death, is rarely assisted suicide. *Facilitated* suicide literally is assisted suicide according to established concepts, because it requires suicidists to themselves employ death-causing means provided. *Enabled* suicide is more problematic, ranging from individuals activating death-causing devices tailored to their situations, to perhaps no more than saying something like "Do it now" to an assisting physician.[21] What mostly goes on in our hospitals, and what will certainly increase in frequency, is not assisted suicide in either of these senses. Patients are seldom provided with fatal dosages for their own use, and fewer have death-enabling devices set up for them to activate. Instead what we are dealing with is something new: elective death achieved through synergistic cooperation between patients and physicians. Managed death seems to be neither assisted suicide nor voluntary euthanasia. Obviously, both assisted suicide and euthanasia occur in medical contexts, but these are the exceptions and are usually newsworthy. The standard practice is something different. Mostly it consists of changes in treatment, such as cessation of administration of antibiotics, even failing to turn an elderly patient in bed to prevent pooling of liquid in the lungs. These changes may be done with patients' knowledge and concurrence, but they may be done on *assumption* of concurrence—and then thought of and justified as lending assistance in suicide. This is what makes it imperative that we better understand managed death and not minimize the moral responsibility of those who provide it by allocating that responsibility to patients.

1.   As mentioned, I do not care for the phrase "managed death," but it has the advantage of greater neutrality than alternatives.

2.   Senate, 1995: 11.

3.   1964 (New York: Simon and Schuster).

4.   Narveson, 1986: 58.

5.   Sandel, 1997: 27.

6.   *Webster's Unabridged* (Random House Electronic edition) defines the relevant sense of "synergism" as "2. the joint action of agents...that when taken together increase each other's effectiveness."

7.   Stolberg, 1998, my emphasis.

8.   Beauchamp, 1980.

9.   The first recorded case of assisted suicide under Oregon's new law took place on March 25, 1998. In *The New York Times* story on the case, it was stressed that the Oregon law permits physicians to *prescribe* lethal doses of barbiturates, etc., but prohibits them from *administering* the medication. It also merits mention that whatever one thinks of Dr. Kevorkian's practices, his "death machine" must be activated by the suicidist.

10.   I owe this case to Alistair Macleod.

11.   I owe this case to Christine Overall.

12.   I owe this formulation to Alistair Macleod.

13.   This was the so-called "Eichmann defense."

14.   In a letter regarding an early version of this paper. Caplan is the director of the University of Pennsylvania's bioethics institute.

15.   Of course their intentions may be ill-conceived, but the point is that death would ensue entirely from the suicidist's own intentions.

16.   Kristol, 1993.

17.   Kristol, 1993.

18.   Prado, 1998.

19.   I add "significant" to modify "coercion" because there is always a measure of *contextual* coercion in circumstances where suicide is considered and possibly committed.

20.   As implied earlier, death's protraction need not involve elaborate technology. The terminally ill and the very elderly may be kept alive long after they would otherwise have died with fairly uncomplicated treatment. The paradigm is aggressive treatment of the pneumonia that is often contracted in the final stages of terminal illness and advanced age.

21.   Incapacitated patients might be only able to, say, blink their eyes to indicate readiness, but the point is that they still control the actions of those assisting, in contrast to provision of euthanasia where the person performing euthanasia controls the timing of death.

Sandra J. Taylor

SIMPLY CALLING A TELEPHONE AN ELEPHANT WON'T DO

———

Assisted suicide and euthanasia are "bad" words in the practical world of health care. If a practitioner allows that active aid-in-dying of the sort connoted by these terms ought to be allowed in certain circumstances, he or she is very often looked at by colleagues as being morally questionable. This is in part because assisted suicide and euthanasia are legally prohibited and therefore assumed to be morally wrong. As well, many major religions prohibit suicide, assisted suicide and euthanasia.

The result has been twofold. First, there is a real reluctance to look at both sides of the debate concerning both the conceptual differences (or non-differences) between what clinicians do every day and what we perceive to be assisted suicide and euthanasia, and the moral discussion concerning the rightness or wrongness of active aid-in-dying. Generally health care practitioners are not interested in the conceptual analysis that helps clarify motives, intentions and the definition of actions. And that is understandable. That is the job of the philosopher or other theoretician, not the clinician...or at least traditionally that has been the case. But, second, euthanasia and assisted suicide have, for historical reasons, acquired the connotation of moral wrongness. Health care providers, like most in society, set out to do what they believe to be right. We believe that giving increasing doses of sedation

———

to a terminally ill, suffering individual is right, whether or not she might die sooner because of it than she might have otherwise. To sedate and remove a competent person from the ventilator at his request is viewed as right because of our emphasis on respect for an individual's self-determination. But the vocabulary of assisted suicide and euthanasia cannot be used to describe these actions, because these actions are right and assisted suicide and euthanasia are wrong. Therefore, it is argued and assumed, whatever is going on cannot be assisted suicide and euthanasia. Medical practitioners will say that they are just withdrawing treatment to allow the underlying disease to take its course. Or they will say that the sedation they are giving a dying patient is to alleviate suffering, not to kill the patient. And the fact is, both statements are correct. However, that may not change the fact that assistance of this sort in the dying process may linguistically and conceptually fit the definition of assisted suicide and euthanasia.

The moral conundrum then becomes whether or not some instances of assisted suicide and euthanasia may be morally right and if they may, why will we not allow a competent, terminally ill person, but one who is not attached to a machine, to have active assistance in dying. And if they may not, how do we justify helping people die by sedating them and removing them from ventilators or not putting feeding tubes in their stomachs when that is all that is keeping them from living for many months or years. And how do we justify not resuscitating a patient in the final stages of ALS who has attempted suicide.

For nearly a decade I have practiced as a clinical ethicist in a large acute care teaching hospital where much of my work has centered on end-of-life decision making. In this paper I would like to look at the common end-of-life practices in health care today. Are they fundamentally distinguishable from definitions of assisted suicide and euthanasia? Whereas it is not my intent in this short paper to answer this question definitively, I will suggest by examples that it is not obvious that there is a clear distinction between these practices and what we define as assisted suicide and euthanasia. It may be that our ever increasing emphasis on both respect for self-determination and the technological suspension of death results in health care providers unwittingly being put into situations where they are participating in actions in which the law simply does not jibe with practice. When law is in place that seems counter to actions that are generally perceived to be right and that are done routinely, a dichotomy exists that requires a serious look.

The fundamental questions are two. First, is there a basic and articulable difference between those actions believed by physicians and others to be right (withdrawing treatment and increasing amounts of sedation) and those actions believed to be wrong (assisted suicide and euthanasia)? And, second, if we cannot find and articulate this difference, are we left with the conclusion that there may be times when assisted suicide and euthanasia may be morally right? Definitions ought not to be used merely as moral suasion. Definitions must fit the actions in question.

Philosopher Tom Beauchamp says a person commits suicide if:

1. That person intentionally brings about his or her own death.

2. Others do not coerce him or her to do the action; and

3. Death is caused by conditions arranged by the person for the purpose of bringing about his or her own death.[1]

Assisted suicide is defined by the Special Senate Committee on Assisted Suicide and Euthanasia as *the act of killing oneself intentionally with the assistance of another who provides the means, the knowledge, or both.*[2]

With these definitions in mind, consider the case of Mr. B. W., a 40-year-old man who was admitted to the ICU of a tertiary care center with a self-inflicted gunshot wound to his head. He was intubated, ventilated and given numerous medications for his blood pressure. As well, Mr. B. W. had developed a coagulopathy (his blood would not clot and therefore his bleeding would not stop), so he was being continuously transfused. Shortly after his admission, members of his family found notes to the effect that some months ago he had been told of his diagnosis of a universally fatal disease. The disease is progressive, with physical and mental deterioration ultimately culminating in premature death. In the notes he asked that if he was to be found alive that no resuscitative measures be taken. According to his family and his physician he was not clinically depressed. The family asked that treatment be withdrawn, the patient was moved from the ICU to a room and allowed to die. The wishes of the patient as articulated by his substitute decision maker(s) were honored and he died. Although it is possible that he could have survived, his quality of life would have been significantly impaired and it would only get worse. Both because of the gunshot wound and his progressive disease, the health care team were comfortable that they had done the right thing by withdrawing treatment and allowing him to die. There can be no doubt that Mr. B. W. intended to commit suicide. It is also the case that we participated in completing his suicide. The question then becomes, was this a case of assistance in suicide, given that Mr. B. W. could have survived with help. Did we provide the means and knowledge? Certainly we did not provide the gun but neither did we provide the help that could have had him survive. Our negative act resulted in his death, albeit due to his underlying pathology.

In a similar vein, Ms. M. was admitted to the same tertiary care center because of an unsuccessful suicide attempt. It became apparent to the intensivists who were looking after her that there was a "window" in which either care could be withdrawn within hours and the patient be allowed to die, or she would survive but, because of severe brain damage, her survival would only be biological. That is, she would certainly not be able to experience stimuli or communicate. She would live in a persistive vegetative state. After discussion with her family, it was decided that she be sedated, extubated and allowed to die. The justification was that this person would not want to survive in such a state, nor did her family believe it would be proper. Generally our society feels that we need not sustain life when it is clear that no interaction with others is or will be possible, this belief being upheld by religious and secular alike. However, was this assisting her suicide? Given that she could have and most probably would have survived, was this euthanasia?

Euthanasia is defined by the Special Senate Committee on Euthanasia and Assisted Suicide as *the deliberate act undertaken by one person with the intention of ending the life of another person in order to relieve that person's suffering where that act is the cause of death.*[3]

In the instance discussed above, the intention, it seems to me, was indeed to "[end] the life of another person," albeit for compassionate motives.

Nancy B., a famous case in Canadian jurisprudence, describes the situation of a young woman left quadriplegic and dependent on a respirator because of a viral disease affecting the nervous system. Over the space of two years she asked repeatedly to be taken off the respirator and allowed to die. Ultimately Nancy B. asked the court to direct the hospital to allow her physician to follow her wishes. The court ruled in her favor and instructed those caring for her that she be given enough sedation that she need not suffer while dying of suffocation. Nancy B. was sedated, the respirator was removed and she died. The argument here would be that the "intention" was not to kill Nancy B. but to follow her wishes and allow her to die. But as American philosopher Dan Brock and others have argued, to suggest that I do not intend something which is bound to happen and I know will happen is a difficult argument to make successfully.[4] And as Beauchamp has suggested, the claim depends on a very narrow conception of what constitutes intentionality.[5] Since Nancy B. was not able to disconnect herself from the ventilator, nor able to sedate herself, the actions of the health professionals could be described, given the above definition, as participating in voluntary euthanasia. Nancy B. asked for and received active aid-in-dying. Sue Rodriguez, on the other hand, was not allowed this help (although it was given outside of existing law) because she was not yet attached to a ventilator, although this would have been inevitable had she continued to live. Two questions may legitimately be asked. First, why does the ventilator *per se* make a difference in the rightness or wrongness of active aid-in-dying and, second, in terms of applying the above stated definition of euthanasia, surely the presence or absence of a ventilator ought to be moot.

The following two situations do not usually find their way into the court system but will be very familiar to health professionals. Whereas these examples are not usually thought of as examples of assisted suicide or euthanasia they do fulfill the definitional requirements set out by Beauchamp and the Senate Committee. The fact that they are situations of terminal illness and take place in a hospital setting do not, I would suggest, obviously change the definition of what is going on.

Ms. Y. was admitted to the ICU in respiratory distress, intubated and ventilated. She had a differential diagnosis of very severe pneumonia or end stage lung cancer. The lab reports confirmed the latter diagnosis and Ms. Y. was told. It was apparent that if she were to continue to survive it would be with the assistance of the respirator. She chose not to live her life in that fashion and asked to have it removed. Her family and physicians agreed, the family spent time with her, she was sedated and extubated, and she died.

Mr. A. was paralyzed and unable to speak or swallow as a result of a stroke. His wife refused the surgical implantation of a feeding tube on his behalf because of his previously expressed verbal and written wishes. The feeding tube was not inserted, he, too, was sedated, and died within three days.

Mr. P. had been married for 45 years when his wife died two years previously. He had visited her grave every week since her death. He suffered a stroke that left him very weak on one side. He was able to get around in a wheelchair, and although he could not speak, his cognitive function was not impaired and he could communicate well. Mr. P. wanted very much to be with his wife. He had a strong religious belief that he would be reunited with her after death and decided he would stop eating and drinking. After much discussion with Mr. P. and his family, the health care providers looking after him were willing to support him and his family in this decision. His meals were brought to him as usual and help was offered in feeding him. He refused food and most fluids, was not forced to eat or drink and died about two weeks later.

An act may be positive or negative. That is, deciding to *do* something, like giving sedation, is a positive act while deciding *not* to do something, like not inserting a feeding tube or not forcing someone to eat, is a negative act. In all of these examples, both the negative acts of not putting in a feeding tube or not feeding orally and the positive act(s) of sedating and removing the respirator resulted in the death of the persons involved. In the cases of Mr. A. and Mr. P., a stroke necessitated a feeding tube for proper nutrition, but that was easily rectified. It was the lack of proper nutrition that caused their death, not the stroke *per se*. Ms. Y. could not breathe without the respirator and although she would have most probably died fairly soon anyway, the withdrawal of the respirator resulted in her death sooner than would have otherwise been the case.

I have chosen these examples for a number of reasons. First, anyone working in health care will recognize them as being common. And, second, they seem to me to be examples of compassionate and right actions. The determination of the rightness or wrongness of an action can be achieved in a number of ways. Usually we look to our duties to alleviate suffering and follow the wishes of the patient. We look to the consequences of our actions: Would a balance of good over bad be achieved? In health care, we consider what the caring thing to do would be. But as well as the morality, it is important to try and analyze these situations from conceptual and definitional perspectives.

If I am dependent on a respirator because of an illness, it seems odd to argue that pulling my ventilator off so that I suffocate is not suicide, while swallowing 30 pills so that my heart stops is. If I am dependent on a respirator because of an illness, it seems odd to argue that sedating me and taking me off the ventilator so that I suffocate is not euthanasia, and injecting potassium chloride so that my heart stops is. If I am dependent on a respirator because of an illness, it seems odd to argue that asking to be sedated and have the ventilator removed so that I suffocate is right, and asking to have an injection of potassium chloride so that my heart stops is wrong. And, as was the case with Sue Rodriguez, if I am not yet dependent on a respirator, but will certainly become so, it seems odd to suggest that I may not ask for assistance in dying, but that as soon as I need to be intubated I may either refuse intubation, be sedated and die or accept intubation, be sedated, be extubated and die. It is important to look at these situations. Whereas there may indeed be psychological differences among the actions we see as being different, those believed to be right and those believed to be wrong, those believed to be suicide or assisted suicide or euthanasia and those believed to be merely withholding or withdrawing treatment, it is important to realize that a psychological difference does not necessarily translate into a conceptual or moral difference.

Years ago when I was a young nurse working in critical care areas, we believed patients ought not to be removed from the ventilator once treatment of that sort had been started as doing so would be killing our patient. This resulted in an obvious conundrum. We could not ventilate people indefinitely but it was felt to be both morally and legally wrong to stop life sustaining treatment. Indeed, a section of the Criminal Code of Canada still speaks to the fact that once treatment has been started it ought not to be stopped if that stoppage will result in the death of the patient. But, of course, it ultimately has to happen, patients cannot be sustained indefinitely, even on respirators. The result was that they were taken off respirators, but it was done surreptitiously, often at night when no one was around. It would be that the respirator simply was no longer attached to the endotracheal tube. In the 1980's my mother-in-law asked repeatedly that her "treatments" be stopped and she be allowed to die of her metastatic cancer. She was simply refused and ultimately was attached to a respirator after having a tracheotomy performed against her will. As a result, her dying process was prolonged with much suffering. However, times have changed. Analyses of such traditional distinctions as withholding and withdrawing treatment have resulted in our understanding that the very same reasons one might never start treatment are the reasons one might stop treatment once it has been started. As well, the emphasis of health care has changed from a very paternalistic endeavor to one in which an individual has more say in what happens to his or her body. As a result, we now *feel* much more comfortable withdrawing treatment when it is no longer believed to be efficacious and we feel better about not forcing treatment on anyone who does not want it. That is, the psychological distinction has changed given the conceptual and moral analysis of the past years. But we still feel that there is something "more wrong" with giving an injection of potassium chloride than with increasing sedation of a patient until he or she dies. And there may be something fundamentally different definitionally and morally, but a psychological distinction is not, in and of itself, definitive. It doesn't *necessarily* make it so.

It is often suggested that the difference is in the fact that one is doing something positive to bring about a death with an injection. In moral terms, to do something positive to bring about a death is not *necessarily* wrong any more than to omit to do something is *necessarily* right. If a physician could easily treat a life-threatening event but neglects to do so and the patient dies, then the physician could be culpable, morally and legally. Her actions could be described as murder *or* euthanasia/withholding treatment depending on the context in which the actions were taken. The morality of these kinds of situations for the individual will depend on things like what does the patient want, what is the prognosis and how can we alleviate suffering. Again, the emphasis on intention will not help here. If the physician allowed the patient to die against his will because she would inherit his money or could not be bothered treating him, she would be committing murder. One the other hand, if her motive was to alleviate suffering and her patient did not want to continue to live, she would be participating in "withholding treatment" or, I would suggest, by definition she would be participating in euthanasia. Her *motive* was to inherit money in the first instance and to follow the wishes of her patient in the second. Her *intention* in both scenarios was to withhold treatment knowing death would occur as a result. This distinction is important and ought not to be blurred to define an action inappropriately. The fact that we do not like the sound of euthanasia does not change its definition.

As well, the definitional difference cannot be justified simply by saying it is so. The fact that I call my telephone an elephant does not make it an elephant. The fact that we call an injection of potassium chloride euthanasia and failure to put in a feeding tube something else, does not make it so. As well, because of our increasingly sophisticated treatment modalities, physicians and nurses are sometimes put in the position of having to be very aggressive if they are going to allow their patient to die peacefully. Now it may be that we ought to be looking at the aggressive nature of treatment and the emphasis we put on such treatments. Perhaps we ought to rethink the weight we have given to the self-determining patient who may or may not be able to be truly informed of their treatment decisions. Maybe we should be looking at advance directives, and assessing whether or not we can really understand treatment decisions of the sort we are being asked to make before the fact, particularly if it is our lawyer and not our doctor with whom we are discussing these options. And it is clear that we ought to be lobbying for more and better palliative care in our health care system.

However, none of these things change the original point. Definitionally and morally it is not obvious that there is a *bone fide* fundamental difference between what we do on a daily basis in our institutions and what our laws prohibit us from doing. It may be that fear of the "slippery slope" is such that at this time we want to say that we just don't want to move any further in decriminalizing or legalizing active aid-in-dying, that is, assisted suicide or euthanasia. But we should at least acknowledge that this is what is going on. To call the assistance we give to dying people "merely withholding or withdrawing treatment" or "merely sedating to alleviate suffering" seems to be a definitional distortion. Simply calling a telephone an elephant won't do.

1. Beauchamp, 1980: 77.
2. Senate, 1995.
3. Senate, 1995.
4. Brock, 1989: 349–351.
5. Beauchamp and Childress, 1989: 130.

Russell Savage

DEATH AND THE LAW

Considering the problem of dying in the medical context from the standpoint of Canadian law, it is helpful to discuss a series of contrasts or distinctions. The first distinction is between active euthanasia[1] and assisted suicide. The second is a distinction between euthanasia and assisted suicide on the one hand, as opposed to hastening death as a consequence of alleviating suffering by withholding life-prolonging medical procedures or as an incident of pain-reducing palliative care on the other hand. The third contrast is between assisted suicide and covert euthanasia. In this context I shall argue that assisted suicide cannot be restricted to situations where the patient facilitates his or her own death through some direct action. Under the legal doctrine of *parties*, situations where a person's death is facilitated by a second party on instructions from a patient who, for whatever reason, does not physically contribute to the process can also count as assisted suicide rather than covert euthanasia. Finally, I will discuss the rationale of keeping assisted suicide as a crime when attempted suicide *per se* is no longer a crime.

I. Euthanasia versus Assisted Suicide

(i) Euthanasia as Murder

Assuming that euthanasia, by definition, involves the intentional bringing about of a person's death, it falls squarely into the primary definition of murder in the *Criminal Code* as contained in section 229.

229. Culpable homicide is murder

(a) where the person who causes the death of a human being

(i) means to cause his death, or

(ii) means to cause him bodily harm that he knows is likely to cause his death, and is reckless whether death ensues or not.

If the act of euthanasia was planned and deliberate it is first-degree murder under section 231(2)[2] and subject to the penalty of life in jail without eligibility for parole until 25 years are served (section 745(a)). In fact, most cases of euthanasia in the medical context would be first-degree murder since the act would, of practical necessity, have to be preceded by some deliberation and planning. It is hard to imagine a doctor carrying out an act of mercy killing on the "spur of the moment" without some forethought and planning. There is no provision in the *Criminal Code* to distinguish killing motivated by an intent to end suffering.

(ii) Assisted Suicide

Assisted suicide is a separate offence from murder with a different penalty:

241. Every one who

(a) counsels a person to commit suicide, or

(b) aids or abets a person to commit suicide, whether suicide ensues or not, is guilty of an indictable offence and liable to imprisonment for a term not exceeding fourteen years.

Note that the crime of assisted suicide is not even in the continuum under culpable homicide from manslaughter through to first-degree murder.[3]

II. Active Euthanasia and Assisted Suicide versus Death Hastening Treatment

Ending of a patient's suffering *by* causing death (active euthanasia or suicide) is distinguished from the situation where death is a side effect of some action or omission intended to alleviate suffering (passive euthanasia). For example, a doctor might refrain from heroic life-prolonging measures, usually after consultation with the patient and/or a surrogate. A second example would be a situation where palliative care intended to ease patient suffering also hastens death. In both these cases the law is clear that the physician is not involved in any sort of culpable homicide or other offence.

This was confirmed in the *Rodriguez* case from the Supreme Court of Canada where Sopinka J., writing for the majority, stated that in cases where the doctor discontinues treatment at the direction of the patient, the doctor is not assisting in the patient's suicide even if both the doctor and the patient know that such discontinuance will hasten the onset of death:

> Whether or not one agrees that the active vs. passive distinction is maintainable, however, the fact remains that under our common law, the physician has no choice but to accept the patient's instructions to discontinue treatment. To continue to treat the patient when the patient has withdrawn consent to that treatment constitutes battery (Ciarlariello and Nancy B., *supra*). The doctor is therefore not required to make a choice that will result in the patient's death, as he would be if he chose to assist a suicide or to perform active euthanasia.[4]

Sopinka J. also makes the related point that there is no culpable homicide when palliative care is given to ease pain even when it has the known effect of hastening death:

> The fact that doctors may deliver palliative care to terminally ill patients without fear of sanction, it is argued, attenuates to an even greater degree any legitimate distinction which can be drawn between assisted suicide and what are currently acceptable forms of medical treatment. The administration of drugs designed for pain control in dosages which the physician knows will hasten death constitutes active contribution to death by any standard. However, the distinction drawn here is one based

upon intention—in the case of palliative care the intention is to ease pain, which has the effect of hastening death, while in the case of assisted suicide, the intention is undeniably to cause death. The Law Reform Commission, although it recommended the continued criminal prohibition of both euthanasia and assisted suicide, stated, at p. 70 of the Working Paper, that a doctor should never refuse palliative care to a terminally ill person only because it may hasten death. In my view, distinctions based upon intent are important, and in fact form the basis of our criminal law. While factually the distinction may, at times, be difficult to draw, legally it is clear. The fact that in some cases, the third party will, under the guise of palliative care, commit euthanasia or assist in suicide and go unsanctioned due to the difficulty of proof cannot be said to render the existence of the prohibition fundamentally unjust.[5]

Although the distinction here is rather fine and perhaps difficult to draw in practice, it is conceptually clear from a legal point of view. A fundamental precept of criminal law is that for an act to be *criminal*, it must have two components. The technical legal terms for these components are *actus reus* and *mens rea*. The *actus reus* is the physical aspect of the action and the *mens rea* is the so-called "mental element." This is sometimes referred to as the intentional aspect of the action. An example of this would be a situation where the "physical" act is hitting another person in the face by slamming a door on him/her. If the perpetrator slammed the door with the intention of hitting the victim, then the action would be the crime of assault.[6] If, on the other hand, the perpetrator did not see the victim before the act and had no intention to hit anybody but was only meaning to shut the door, there would be no assault because the necessary *mens rea* for the crime of assault was not present. In common terms we would say that there was no assault because hitting the victim was "just an accident." For the crime of assault there must be the physical act of the application of force upon another person without their consent (the *actus reus* of the assault) and this application of force must be intentional in that the perpetrator would have to *mean* to strike the victim (the *mens rea* of the assault).[7] This analysis of actions as composed of the *actus reus* and the *mens rea* facilitates the distinction between causing death to alleviate suffering and causing death as a by-product of efforts to alleviate suffering. If a doctor kills a patient to end his or her suffering, then there is the *actus reus* of killing the patient by some means or another and the *mens rea* of intending or meaning to kill the patient. The laudable purpose of the killing does not lessen the culpability so long as the action was an intentional killing. If, on the other hand, a doctor decides, probably in consultation with the patient and/or the next of kin, to lessen suffering by removing artificial life support or by administering drugs to lessen pain that may also shorten life, we do not have the same *mens rea* as before. The *actus reus* of the killing is present in that something is done to the patient that hastens death. The *mens rea* here though does not involve killing but only the alleviation of suffering. A similar analysis is appropriate in a situation where the patient directs that a particular medical procedure be stopped. In both of the latter situations the doctor does not "mean" to kill the patient as in the case where the killing itself is what is intended. This distinction holds even if in both sorts of cases the doctor is aware that his/her actions will have the effect of hastening death.

III. Assisted Suicide versus Covert Euthanasia

As discussed, both active euthanasia *and* assisted suicide (of any kind) are clearly crimes under Canadian law. Since both would incur legal culpability, the practical distinction between the two is the difference in potential penalty; a life term for euthanasia (as murder) and a maximum of 14 years for assisted suicide. This differential in potential penalty provides a motive to characterize an action as assisted suicide when it is really covert euthanasia.[8] There is some utility, therefore, to properly characterize the distinction between assisted suicide and covert euthanasia.

There is a distinction to be drawn between assisted suicide and covert euthanasia; however, this distinction cannot be drawn on the basis of whether or not the patient was directly involved in bringing about his or her death. At law, it is entirely possible for a doctor to be assisting the patient to commit suicide even if the death was brought about some time after the patient is beyond any ability to participate in bringing on his or her death. To understand how this is possible, it is necessary to refer to the legal notion of *parties*.

Section 21 of the *Criminal Code* reads:

21. (1) Everyone is a party to an offence who

    (a) actually commits it;

    (b) does or omits to do anything for the purpose of aiding any person to commit it;

or

    (c) abets any person in committing it.

(2) Where two or more persons form an intention in common to carry out an unlawful purpose and to assist each other therein and any one of them, in carrying out the common purpose, commits an offence, each of them who know or ought to have known that the commission of the offence would be a probable consequence of carrying out the common purpose is a party to that offence.

The concept of *party* as expressed by section 21 above would deny a relevant distinction between situations where the patient is directly (physically) responsible for his own death with the aid of the doctor and those where, on prior instructions from the patient, the doctor brings about the death of the patient without any direct input from the patient. In the latter sort of situation the doctor would be a *party* to the patient's suicide. This would still be qualitatively different from the doctor killing the patient without consultation with the patient because the doctor (and possibly others) decided that it was time for the patient to be put out of his suffering. That would be a clear case of euthanasia. If the doctor was carrying out the patient's express wishes as in the *Rodriguez* case where the patient arranged for herself to be killed when she was no longer able to function and do anything including giving the final go ahead for the act of killing[9] then, according to the *parties* doctrine, the doctor would be participating in the act of suicide. The legal concept of *parties* is that the party is just as guilty of (responsible for) the act in question as if he/she committed it directly.[10]

Nevertheless, it is still possible to make the distinction between assisted suicide and covert euthanasia. In the legal context the distinction is between acting on the direction of the patient so that the doctor is, in fact, acting as the patient's agent, as opposed to deciding that the patient should die without reference to any expressed direction from the patient. It is this absence of direction from the patient that is key. An act of killing is murder even if it is truly an act of *mercy killing* done out of compassion for the patient if the decision to perform the act was taken by the doctor without reference to any direction from the patient, past or present.

IV. The Rationale of Assisted Suicide as a Party Offence

A peculiar feature of the legal sanction against assisted suicide is that it is no longer illegal for a person to attempt to commit suicide,[11] yet it is a crime for another person to assist in that person's attempt. The usual way of characterizing the sort of case where somebody is guilty of a crime as a party, is to see the guilt of the party as dependent on the guilt (or at least potential guilt) of the principle in the crime in question. For instance, if the principle sets out to commit a murder, his or her assistant would also be guilty of murder or attempted murder by virtue of the assistance. The principle would be guilty of murder or attempted murder and the assistant would be guilty of the same thing as a party. With respect to the crime of assisted suicide, however, the only offence is that of being a party to the act of suicide. As mentioned above, the principle in this case is not committing a crime. In other words, it is legal to try to kill yourself but illegal for somebody to help you do it.

The only means of making sense of this is to assume that the policy behind the proscription against assisted suicide is an abhorrence of the act of suicide even though it is no longer a crime. In the *Rodriguez* case Sopinka J. goes to great lengths to demonstrate that it is a fundamental societal policy to discourage the taking of life:

Section 241(b) has as its purpose the protection of the vulnerable who might be induced in moments of weakness to commit suicide. This purpose is grounded in the state interest in protecting life and reflects the policy of the state that human life should not be depreciated by allowing life to be taken. This policy finds expression not only in the provisions of our Criminal Code which prohibit murder and other violent acts against others notwithstanding the consent of the victim, but also in the policy against capital punishment and, until its repeal, attempted suicide. This is not only a policy of the state, however, but is part of our fundamental conception of the sanctity of human life.[12]

This policy was seen by him to be so fundamental that the prohibition against assisted suicide must be absolute lest the door be left open for suffering patients to be persuaded to end their lives when they are at their weakest both physically and mentally. The implication is clear that even though the attempt to commit suicide is no longer actually a crime, the Law is still at pains to discourage it.

This is not the only instance where Parliament has demonstrated disapproval of certain kinds of actions without making the actions themselves illegal. Examples are prostitution and the sale and distribution of tobacco products. While prostitution itself is not illegal, most of the activities surrounding it are, such as communicating for the purpose, operating a bawdyhouse and pimping. Likewise, the sale and distribution of tobacco products is still legal though there are severe restrictions on advertising and corporate sponsorship of arts and sporting events as well as onerous requirements for health warnings on the packaging of tobacco products.

We can see then that the removal of the legal *sanction* against suicide did not remove the legal *disapproval* of the act. It is on this basis that the majority in *Rodriguez* denied the application for a constitutional exemption in the case of a dying patient attempting to arrange for a managed death at a time in the future when that patient would no longer be competent to participate in the killing. If the killing is intrinsically to be eschewed by Society, and hence the Law, then one should not be surprised at the failure of arguments that there is some injustice in the fact that suffering patients are unable to have assistance in committing suicide even though if they could do it by themselves, it would not technically be a crime.

1. "Active euthanasia" refers to the intentional killing of a person to alleviate that person's suffering. This is opposed to "passive euthanasia," which is the hastening or causing of death indirectly as a consequence of an act or omission that has a purpose other than the death of the person. From this point on, I will use the term "euthanasia" to refer to what is meant by the phrase "active euthanasia."

2. 231(1). Murder is first-degree murder or second-degree murder. Murder is first-degree murder when it is planned and deliberate.

3. S. 231(1) through 234 indicate that culpable homicide involves first- and second-degree murder, infanticide and manslaughter.

4. *Re Rodriguez and Attorney-General of British Columbia et al.* (1993) 85 C.C.C. (3d) 15 (S.C.C.), at 77, 78.

5. *Ibid.*, at 78.

6. Actually it would be either assault with a weapon (s. 267(a) of the *Code*) or, if there was an injury, assault causing bodily harm (s. 267(b)).

7. S. 265(1)(a) of the *Criminal Code*.

8. For the purposes of this discussion, "covert euthanasia" refers to an act of euthanasia that is not readily apparent *as* euthanasia.

9. Note that in the *Rodriguez* case, starvation would not have been an option for the patient since at the relevant time she would be fed intravenously and be unable to communicate in any way.

10. In *R. v. Thatcher* (1987) 32 C.C.C. (3d) 48 (S.C.C.), the accused, Colin Thatcher, was convicted of the first-degree murder of his wife even though there was evidence indicating that he may have had nothing to do with his wife's killing directly. The indication was that he directed another person to carry it out so that he would be able to avail himself of an alibi.

11. Attempted suicide was a crime listed in the *Criminal Code* until it was repealed in 1972.

12. *Re Rodriguez (supra* n. 4), at 69.

Eike-Henner W. Kluge

ASSISTED SUICIDE, ETHICS AND THE LAW

The Implications of Autonomy and Respect for Persons, Equality and Justice, and Beneficence

---

Introduction

The *Criminal Code* of Canada, as indeed the relevant codes of many jurisdictions, prohibits assisted suicide. This prohibition is contained in section 241(b), which states that

> 241. Every one who...(b) aids or abets a person to commit suicide, whether suicide ensues or not, is guilty of an indictable offence and liable to imprisonment for a term not exceeding fourteen years.

There are various reasons for this prohibition. One of them is to deter unscrupulous persons from advancing their own ends by aiding or abetting clinically depressed individuals, those of limited intelligence or individuals who are otherwise *non compos mentis*. Another is the value that society places on human life—a value that, in the eyes of the law makers, might easily be eroded if assistance in committing suicide were to be decriminalized.[1]

Unquestionably, these are important aims that deserve legal advancement. Nevertheless, to enshrine them in legislation such as section 241(b) is inappropriate because to do so violates three ethical principles that are fundamental to a free and democratic society: the principle of autonomy and respect for persons, the principle of equality and justice, and the principle of beneficence. The discussion that follows shows how this is

---

83

the case. It concludes with a brief sketch of model legislation that would adhere to these principles while safeguarding legitimate societal interests. The discussion will be phrased in reference to the case of *Rodriguez*[2] to show how the violation of these ethical principles plays out in actual terms.

For those unfamiliar with the *Rodriguez* case, Sue Rodriguez was a woman who suffered from amyotrophic lateral sclerosis (ALS).[3] Like all ALS sufferers, Ms. Rodriguez faced the certain expectation that there would come a time when she would be unable to do anything for herself and when she would depend on others not only for her continued care, feeding and personal hygiene, but also breathing itself. While in some cases, ALS sufferers may live for decades and, when appropriately supported, continue to function at a relatively high level, this was not the case with Ms. Rodriguez. She had an acute form of ALS that is associated with a short life expectancy. Ms. Rodriguez had decided, on the basis of settled values centering in her conception of the dignity of the person, that she did not wish to experience the end-stage of her disease. She held that the physical debility and dependence that she would experience as the disease progressed, as well as the attendant physical deterioration, would violate her values and her concept of the dignity of the person. She therefore wished to end her life before reaching this stage, and she claimed this as a right. Moreover, she argued, in opposition to section 241(b) of the *Criminal Code,* that this right included the right to assistance in committing suicide. She phrased her claim in reference to the three ethical principles that have already been mentioned.[4]

Principle of Autonomy and Respect for Persons

The foundation for her argument was laid by an appeal to the principle of autonomy and respect for persons. This principle may be phrased as follows: *Everyone has the right to self-determination subject only to an unjust infringement on the equal and competing rights of others.*[5] The principle is integral to a free and democratic society because it underlies the very concept of individual freedom on which such a society is based.

Given the nature of ALS in general and her specific disease process in particular, Ms. Rodriguez had reasonable grounds to believe that when the disease process reached the stage when continued life would offend her values and her sense of dignity, she would be unable to end her own life. In theory, therefore, she had several options: 1. She could wait until the offence against her values and sense of dignity became unbearable and then refuse food and water, thus killing herself through her own inaction without involving the assistance of anyone else. 2. She could actively commit suicide without assistance at some point before her increasing disability prevented her from doing so. 3. She could wait, but only until she could still herself initiate a chain of causation leading to her death and at that point rely on a physician (or other relevant person) to supply her with the relevant means and/or medication that she would then take herself. 4. She could postpone her deliberate death as long as possible, in keeping with her sense of dignity and values, and then request that a physician directly bring about her death by appropriate medical means.

Option 1 entailed that the manner of Ms. Rodriguez' dying would have violated the very principles that grounded her choice of deliberate death in the first instance. That is, the means necessary for carrying out her purpose—starvation and dehydration, with the attendant state of utter dependence and physiological and mental deterioration—would have contradicted the values inherent in the purpose itself.

Option 2 would have involved no such contradiction. Nor, again, would it have been at variance with the law. However, since it was unpredictable at what point she would reach the stage when her disability was at the cusp of violating her sense of dignity while at the same time still allowing her freedom of action, practical exigencies and the indeterminacy inherent in her situation would have meant that she would have had to end her life *before* it in fact became necessary and her own values dictated. Hence alternative 2 would have meant that she would have had to buy her autonomy and dignity at the price of her accelerated and untimely death.

Options 3 and 4 would have avoided these consequences. However, they were ruled out by section 241(b) of the *Criminal Code*. Hence—so her argument—her autonomy was severely infringed. Consequently, so she maintained, section 241(b) violates the principle of autonomy and respect for persons.

Principle of Equality and Justice

While the principle of autonomy laid the foundation for her argument, the central thrust of Rodriguez' challenge was based on the principle of equality and justice. The principle may be expressed as follows: *Everyone should be treated equally, and deviations from equality of treatment are permissible only to achieve equity and justice.*[6]

The point of this principle is that due allowances must be made for differences among persons if these differences would, or would be likely to, prevent the persons from taking equal advantage of important opportunities that are otherwise available to members of society. This principle underpins society's obligation to make due allowances for handicap. Equity employment policies are a nonmedical example of the principle's application.

More importantly for the present context, however, is that the principle also entails that if a rule, law, policy or practice has the effect of preventing someone from taking equal advantage of the opportunities that are otherwise open to members of society, *even without intending to do so*, then that rule, law, policy or practice is constructively discriminatory. By that very token, such a rule, law, policy or practice would violate the principle of equality and justice, its intent notwithstanding.

The application of this principle to the situation in which Ms. Rodriguez found herself was patent: The absence of voluntary motor control is an inevitable aspect of ALS in its later stages. The absence of voluntary motor control, however, is a prima facie handicap. Therefore the absence of voluntary motor control in the later stages of the disease is a handicap of ALS-sufferers.

There is no law that prohibits suicide.[7] The absence of such a law, therefore, means that all members of society who are *compos mentis* have a freedom right to commit suicide at a time of their choosing and in a manner consistent with their personal values. While section 241(b) did not prevent Rodriguez from committing suicide in the manner specified in alternatives 1 and 2 above, these alternatives either violated her values and sense of dignity or forced her to buy her autonomy at the price of an accelerated death. No such choice faced (or faces) persons who are not disabled as was Ms. Rodriguez. Consequently the law insisted on confirming her in her inability to take advantage of opportunities otherwise available to members of society *without providing a compensatory and equitable relief*. The law, therefore, had the effect of discriminating against her on the basis of her handicap. Consequently it violated equality and justice in a constructively discriminatory fashion.

Moreover, the law recognizes that the conscience, beliefs, aspirations and values of an individual shape the life of that person, and that the right to adhere to one's conscience, beliefs, aspirations and values in self-regarding actions is integral to the autonomy of the person in a free and democratic society.[8] The law also agrees that to force individuals into a manner of living that would violate these values, beliefs and aspirations would be to violate their dignity as human persons.[9] Finally, the courts have accepted this even in cases where acting on the relevant beliefs will predictably lead to the person's death.[10] However, the effect of section 241 (b) and related provisions of the *Criminal Code* is that this perspective does not apply to persons in Ms. Rodriguez' position. Therefore section 241(b) institutionalizes an unequal treatment of conscience, beliefs, aspirations and values of persons who are similarly handicapped. Consequently, by mandating such unequal treatment, the law is once more guilty of a violation of equality and justice.

In addition, it should be noted that section 15 of the *Charter of Rights and Freedoms* states,[11]

> Every individual is equal before and under the law and has the right to equal protection and equal benefit of the law without discrimination and, in particular, without discrimination based

on race, national or ethnic origin, colour, religion, sex, age or mental or physical disability.

The *Charter* as such applies to all Canadian people. Canadians, however, are not all the same. They differ in material endowments and position. The *Charter* recognizes this, and section 15 is intended to ensure that such differences do not provide the grounds for discrimination. However, section 241(b) of the *Criminal Code* has the effect of institutionalizing such discrimination in cases of handicap—as with Sue Rodriguez. Consequently, section 241(b) of the *Criminal Code* is not merely ethically objectionable but also violates the equality and justice section of the *Charter*.

Principle of Beneficence

There are two versions of the principle of beneficence: one strong (traditional) and one weak (contemporary). The strong or traditional version maintains that people have an obligation to do good for others where this good is defined by those who do the good, whether the recipients of the act agree with it or not. Physicians traditionally based their actions on this principle when withholding information from their patients, when making nonconsensual therapeutic decisions for their patients or when overruling their patients' wishes "for the sake of the patients themselves."[12] Nowadays, almost without exception, this version of the principle has been condemned as paternalistic and unacceptable.[13] The weak version of the principle, which is more generally accepted, maintains that everyone has an obligation to assist others in advancing their good, where the nature of this good is defined by the individuals whose good is to be advanced, or where this good is consonant with the values of these persons.

Ms. Rodriguez had defined what she considered to be "the good" in terms of values that included her concept of the dignity of the person. These values were not out of keeping with the socially accepted value that suffering should not be protracted beyond the ability of the individual to bear.[14] On this basis, she claimed that the principle of beneficence entitled her to assistance when she found life an unbearable affront to her sense of dignity and her values.

Since life is frequently identified as a basic good, it might be argued by some that instead of entailing assistance in dying, the principle really entailed that she accept palliation.

However, it must be recognized that the suggestion of palliation as a way of dealing with Ms. Rodriguez' request, and as an attempt to honor her kind of perspective, was fundamentally inappropriate. It failed to come to grips with the core of the issue. The issue was not one of pain—of suffering in a physical sense. It was the violation of her values and of her sense of dignity of the person.[15]

That is to say, in general terms, palliation may well assuage the experience of physical pain and discomfort. However, it cannot deal with the suffering that comes from the violation of one's values and one's dignity as a person. The reason is that suffering should not be understood in merely physical terms. Thus, the *Shorter Oxford English Dictionary* includes the notion of distress in its definition of suffering;[16] and as the ethicist Erich Loewy has noted in his book on suffering, suffering has a central psychological component that is essentially different from physical pain.[17] Therefore, suffering may center in the experience of having one's dignity as a person violated, or in the violation of the values that one holds dear. Palliation can deal with the suffering that is thus engendered only by sedating the sufferer to the point that she or he becomes insensate. However, it is illogical as well as morally perverse to suggest that to render the suffering person insensate to the violation of her or his dignity is to deal with the suffering—or with the violation of dignity that gives rise to that suffering.

It was this mental and spiritual component of suffering that was at issue for Ms. Rodriguez—and it is this component of suffering that is at stake for others who share her values. Therefore, the ethically appropriate way to deal with the suffering caused by the violation of her dignity would have been to provide her with options that would allow her to end her suffering in keeping with her competent and legitimate values. Options 3 and 4 would have had this effect. Palliation did not—and by its very nature cannot—achieve the same end.

Section 1 of the *Charter*

It is one thing to show that a particular law is ethically flawed; it is another to craft a law that translates the relevant insights into a workable statute. For what is required is that the ethical considerations that underlie these insights and that are theoretical in nature intersect with the pragmatic considerations that define the framework within which all social legislation must function. In Canada, section 1 of the *Charter* defines the limits within which ethical considerations may function within the overall framework. It reads as follows:

> S. 1. The *Canadian Charter of Rights and Freedoms* guarantees the rights and freedoms set out in it subject to such reasonable limits prescribed by law and as can demonstrably be justified in a free and democratic society.[18]

By its own logic, section 1 of the *Charter* may be engaged only if it can demonstrably be shown that the rights of the majority cannot be satisfied except by overruling some of the rights of the minority. However, this demonstration cannot be achieved by showing that there is a *possibility* that the rights and interests of the majority maybe threatened unless certain individual liberties are suspended, or by arguing that the relevant limitation of rights and freedoms makes for greater *ease of administration.* If that were the case, minority rights could always be violated and the remaining clauses of the *Charter* might just as well not exist. Instead, it must demonstrably be shown that the rights of the majority are in fact threatened in an irresolvable fashion, and that there is no way of accommodating the rights of minority and majority together.

Therefore the test of section 1 is whether it can be shown that no mechanism exists that would allow the rights of the minority to be satisfied without entailing an impossibility of satisfying the rights of the majority. If it can be shown that no such mechanism exists, then section 1 may be engaged; if not, then an application of section 1 must fail. In other words, the *onus probandi* lies on the party claiming validation under section 1. It does not lie on the party who claims a violation of the other sections of the *Charter*.

This condition was not met in the case of *Rodriguez*. The majority reasoning of the Supreme Court stated, but did not demonstrably show, that the section 15 rights of the minority could not be met without making it impossible to meet the rights of the majority—or, for that matter, without opening the floodgates of misuse and abuse of the weak and infirm. In fact, two of Canada's most eminent jurists—Chief Justice Lamer of the Supreme Court of Canada and Chief Justice McEachern of the British Columbia Court of Appeals—suggested ways in which the two could be reconciled. These proposals, duly modified and integrated, may form the basis of appropriate legislation as follows:[19]

Proposed Assisted Suicide Act:

yyy.1 If a person suffers from an incurable and irremediable disease or medical condition, and if that person experiences the disease or condition as violating the fundamental values of that person, then

(a) that person may make application to a superior court for permission to request the assistance of a physician in terminating his life as quickly and as painlessly as possible in keeping with the fundamental values of that person; and

(b) on presentation of evidence by an independent psychiatrist and the attending physician that the person making the request is competent to do so, the court shall hear such a request as expeditiously as possible.

yyy.2 The court, upon due consideration of the mental and physical state of the person requesting permission under yyy.1, and of that person's fundamental values; and taking due account of the medical nature of the affliction of the person requesting such assistance, may grant such an application.

yyy.3 Any permission granted under sec. yyy.2

(a) shall be registered with the regional coroner of the relevant jurisdiction;

(b) shall be for a period of six months; and

(c) shall include an order that there shall be due notification of the coroner if such a permission has been acted upon.

yyy.4 Any physician acting upon a permission under sec. yyy.2 and in accordance with the wishes of the person making the request under yyy.1 shall use such measures as he or she deems, upon due consideration, to be appropriate for assisting that person in terminating her or his life as quickly and painlessly as possible.

yyy.5 Any physician acting upon a permission granted under secs. yyy.2, yyy.3 and yyy.4, and acting in accordance with the provisions set out therein, shall be deemed not to have committed an offence within the meaning of this Act.

yyy.6 Any revocation of a request made by a competent person under sec. yyy.1 shall take immediate effect and shall be deemed to render null and void any previous request made by that person under sec. yyy.1.

Conclusion

The preceding analysis has shown that to permit suicide but to prohibit by criminal sanctions assisted suicide for persons who are unable to kill themselves violates fundamental ethical principles. In *Rodriguez,* the Supreme Court of Canada unanimously agreed that section 241(b) of the *Criminal Code* violates section 15 of the *Charter of Rights and Freedoms.*[20] A bare majority argued that section 15 is saved by section 1. It has been shown that this is not the case: The standards set by section 1 itself for its own engagement were not met in this particular case—and indeed could probably never be met.

It is therefore appropriate to suggest that for the sake of both ethical and juridical consistency, section 241(b) be struck down and legislation similar to what has been outlined be introduced in its place. The proposed legislation would rectify an egregious flaw in the current statutes. At the same time, it would meet the objection that unscrupulous persons might take advantage of the legislation by assisting clinically depressed individuals, those of limited intelligence or persons who are otherwise *non compos mentis*. The role contemplated for the judiciary would leave such a possibility as remote as it is at the present time.

As to the value that society places on human life, the reasoning above has shown that since this societal value has not been allowed to interfere with the competent individual's freedom right to take her or his own life, it would be unethical to allow it to interfere with what should be an equal liberty right on part of persons who are disabled.

1. Special Senate Committee on Euthanasia and Assisted Suicide, *On Life and Death: Report of the Special Senate Committee on Euthanasia and Assisted Suicide* (Ottawa: Minister of Supply and Services, 1995), at 71 *et pass.*

2. *R. v. Rodriguez* [1993] 3 S.C.R. 519.

3. ALS is a degenerative disease of the nervous system. It affects the motor neurons that carry impulses from the brain and spinal cord to the muscles and leads to a degeneration of the muscles themselves. The disease is incurable. It usually results in death within three to 10 years.

4. Strictly speaking, Ms. Rodriguez did not conceive of this approach. The author proposed it to Mr. C. Considine, Ms. Rodriguez' lawyer when, in his capacity as consultant ethicist, he was asked by Mr. Considine how, in his opinion, the suit should be framed. The author also cautioned Mr. Considine against using the *Bland* case—a suggestion that, in contrast to the preceding, Mr. Considine declined to follow.

5. For similar formulations, see Beauchamp and Childress, 1989; Engelhardt, Jr., 1986; Garrett, Baillie and Garrett, 1988; Storch, 1982; Veatch, 1981.

6. *Ibid.*

7. The relevant section of the *Criminal Code* was removed in 1972.

8. *R. v. Morgentaler* [1988] 1 S.C.R. 30.

9. See *Nancy B. V. Hôtel-Dieu* (1992), 86, D.L.R. (4th) 385 (Que. S.C.).

10. *Ibid.*; see also *Malette v. Shulman* [1990] (Ont. C.A.) 72 O.R. (2d) 417 and *re L.D.K.* (1985) R.F.L. (2d) 164.

11. *Constitution Act*, R.S.C. 1985, Appendix II, No. 44 Part VII Schedule B, Part I Sec. 15. (1).

12. The classic statement of a paternalistic approach is Thomas Percival, *Medical Ethics: Or a Code of Institutes and Precepts, Adapted to the Professional*

Conduct of Physicians and Surgeons (London: Russell and Bickerstaff, 1803). The perspective enunciated here was standard in medical codes of ethics all over the world until approximately 20 years ago.

13. See Buchanan, 1978; for a discussion of paternalism from another perspective, see Beauchamp and Childress, 1979: 153–164, who adopt a utilitarian approach. See also Callahan, 1986; Dworkin, 1972; Ellin, 1981; Engelhardt, Jr. 1986: 252–262; Feinberg, 1973: 52; Gert and Culver, 1976: 45–47; Graber, 1981; Kluge, 1992, Chapter 4, "The Physician-Patient Relationship."

14. In this respect, her position was in keeping with the general principle enunciated by Pope John Pius XII in his Allocution to the 1957 International Congress of Anesthesiologists, when he said that one is not morally obligated to use "means that do not involve any grave burden for oneself *or* another. A more strict requirement would be too burdensome for most men and would render the attainment of the higher, more important good too difficult." ["Prolongation of Life: Allocution to an International Congress of Anesthesiologists," Nov. 24, 1957, *Osservatore Romano* 4 (1957) emphasis added.] His Holiness went on to identify what counts as too burdensome as what would be too costly, too painful or very difficult or very dangerous for the person in question. His Holiness would have rejected Ms. Rodriguez' request for assisted suicide; however, the logic of His Holiness' statement goes the other way. Similar remarks apply to the current position of the Catholic Church. See Sacred Congregation for the Doctrine of the Faith, "Declaration on Euthanasia," Vatican City, 1980.

15. Ms. Rodriguez was in a palliative care program provided by Hospice in Victoria.

16. *The Shorter Oxford English Dictionary*, 3rd ed., "suffer: to have something painful, distressing, or injurious inflicted or imposed upon one; to submit to with pain, distress or grief."

17. Loewy, 1991, Chapter 1, "The Nature of Suffering," especially pp. 6–12.

18. *Constitution Act*, R.S.C. 1985, Appendix II, No. 44 Part VII Schedule B, Part I Sec. 1.

19. The proposed legislation is a revised version of what was presented to the Special Senate Committee on Assisted Suicide and Euthanasia. It has since been adopted by the Right to Die Society of Canada.

20. *Loc. cit.*

David Checkland and Michel Silberfeld

DECISION-MAKING CAPACITY AND ASSISTED SUICIDE

———

Decision-making capacity (mental competence) functions, in theory at least, to protect individual freedom from paternalism. Those who possess such capacity in regard to a certain matter are protected from the imposition of well-meaning concern for their well-being. Those who lack such capacity may, if certain further conditions are met, have their decisions overridden by someone appointed to supervise and protect them from their own lack of understanding or inability to appreciate matters. The possibility of liberalizing the law to allow assisted suicide raises important questions, two of which are: 1) "If, when and how are judgments about decisional capacity/incapacity to be raised and justified in such cases?"; 2) "What does and does not get settled by such judgments of capacity?" We will pursue these general questions through discussion of more particular questions they give rise to.

We shall assume without argument for present purposes that: 1) definitions of decision-making capacity in terms of the ability to understand relevant matters and to appreciate the consequences of various options are adequate; 2) a person may be competent to decide some matters and incompetent, at the same time, to decide others; 3) no direct inference is possible from most diagnostic or descriptive categories regarding intelligence, psychic state, neurophysiology and so forth to matters of decisional capacity.

———

Question 1: Have we reason to believe that assessments of capacity to decide about or request assisted suicide would result in consistent or justifiable judgments?

There are two distinct aspects to this. One has to do with the principled or theoretical basis for judgments of capacity. The second has to do with difficulties that can exist in applying or enacting a principled theoretical basis, including that of who is competent to perform such assessment. The first question—roughly, whether there exists a matter of fact to be discovered about any person's capacity to make certain sorts of decision—is too large to address adequately here, but certain more specific matters can be discussed.

Question 1a: Do contexts of assisted suicide raise new or special issues regarding the assessment of decisional capacity?

As has been noted, "The correct initial and repeated evaluation of competency is of the utmost importance when dealing with a patient requesting assisted suicide."[1] False negatives (incorrect findings of incompetence) would generally deny the exercise of autonomy (through imposition of guardianship), thereby depriving persons of their rights and possibly imposing unwanted suffering. False positives (incorrect findings of competence) could implicate those assisting a suicide in unjustifiably killing another.

The very process of assessing a person's capacity can be threatening or demeaning, so when and how the question of competence gets raised is important. Assuming there is usually a fact of the matter to be discerned as to whether or not a certain person lacks or possesses decisional capacity, it remains unclear that anyone has the right to investigate that fact. Rather, she who would assess must justify the need to do so since a person can lose significant rights as a consequence of such an assessment. There is a legal presumption of competence.[2] This means two things: 1) anyone raising the issue of another's decisional capacity must provide reason (usually behavioral evidence) to think that a) the person may lack such capacity and b) the assessment of capacity might benefit the person (by, for instance, leading to the provisions of guardian to supervise relevant decisions); 2) when the evidence regarding a person's capacity is inconclusive the person retains decisional authority. Here we are concerned with 1) rather than 2).

Question 1b: When assisted suicide is at issue, are there special reasons to raise, or not raise, the question of decision-making capacity?

Death's seriousness and irreversibility make it prima facie irrational and against one's interests to choose it. Is that sufficient basis for a general policy of assessing the competence of all who request assisted suicide? We would suggest not. Werth and Liddle (1994) found that 81 percent of their responding psychotherapists believed in the concept of rational suicide. Argument for this possibility is no longer unusual.[3] Laws criminalizing suicide seem archaic. So while the desire to die may make observers *wonder* about capacity and rationality, we would suggest that alone it is insufficient to warrant an assessment (let alone settle the issue of capacity). At least as far as beneficent concern goes, there will need to be some further reason to think a person's decisional capacity possibly compromised.[4]

In cases other than assisted suicide, a further general criterion for a justified assessment is the presence of some danger or risk to the person.[5] When no risk exists it is hard to see how an assessment of capacity could be in a person's interests.[6] It may seem that *ex hypothesi* there is risk[7] where suicide is at issue. But death is usually to be counted a "risk" because it is usually an evil and it is (for the moment) avoidable.[8] It is not obviously a chosen "risk" when it is unavoidable and imminent (as with the terminally ill) since the person cannot here choose *not* to die. So, it will often be next to impossible to apply the condition that we should only assess capacity when there is evidence of risk to the person in cases of requested assistance for suicide. For these reasons, when death is imminent the focus should be on other reasons for calling capacity in question and not on risk. The longer the gap between an expected "natural" death and a proposed suicide, of course, then the greater the possibility that to choose or produce death is to choose an avoidable, hence potentially irrational, evil. There is, therefore, greater need to rely on and consider the issue of risk. (We say "possibility" to allow that even those with long life expectancy may rationally and competently desire death, for example, the much publicized Quebec case of "Nancy B.," a young woman rendered permanently quadriplegic and ventilator-dependent.) Judgments of degree of risk are never value-free. In such cases they are not easily distinguished from the task of settling the value of a person's ongoing life.

So far we have been discussing the role of risk in establishing whether or not a formal assessment of capacity needs to be done. Risk-based approaches to capacity assessment itself have been defended and are rather popular it would seem.[9] On such views, the greater the risk to the agent, the higher the degree of understanding required to possess decisional capacity. It may be that the popularity of such approaches indicates that many will unconsciously "raise the bar" in cases where death is desired. We would suggest that this is to be guarded against. Indeed, the popularity of risk-based views may derive in part from a tendency to confuse the perfectly reasonable demand that assessors of capacity must clearly and carefully justify *their* judgments when death may result, with the quite different demand that the person herself must understand and appreciate more than when alternatives are "safe." Any general tendency to "raise the bar" in cases of desired death could go a long way to frustrating both those wanting to die and the general autonomy-honoring thrust behind moves to liberalize assisted suicide laws.

While alone insufficient to establish incapacity in most cases, behavioral or anecdotal evidence of cognitive deficits, sudden character change or pyschopathology will generally be enough to warrant assessment. If present, such factors can clearly be relevant to a person's ability to understand or appreciate matters.[10] That they appear to be present and might be affecting decisional capacity will generally justify an assessment of capacity.

The assessor's job goes further, of course. The assessor must decide, on the basis of evidence, whether such influences are present and, if so, their relevance to a given person's ability to appreciate and understand the matter in question.[11] Depression will frequently be at issue, both because a desire to die is a characteristic symptom of depression, and because those who are suffering or facing their own death are frequently depressed at some point in the "dying process."[12] Unlike some pathological influences on decision making, depression is frequently treatable. Can we assert the general proposition that "If depression is diagnosed, it should be sufficiently treated until suicidal impulses are controlled or it is found to be untreatable?"[13] We think not. What needs to be established is that such impulses are caused by depression, and are related to deficient capacity. A person may be depressed yet competent. Indeed, depression can be a natural and rational response to one's situation. What needs to be determined in a competency assessment is whether the desire to die is supported by further attitudes that are a person's own, or whether it is produced by forces such as overwhelming depressive feelings or moods that may be beyond a persons' rational control in relevant ways. This can generally be ascertained only by investigating the person's attitudes in some detail and by attending to their history (acquisition, persistence, variability, etc.) and rationality. Finally, there must also be reason to believe that treatment would be successful in removing the desire to die or in restoring the ability to reason about it or act on alternate reasons. If there were reason to believe that treatment could not do these things, or could not do them in time, that would count against offering (let alone imposing) such treatment. With the near-death terminally ill, treatment for depression may face these complications. If it is known in advance that treatment is not likely to work, then a formal assessment of capacity in near-death situations does not seem warranted since the assessment could not result in a benefit for the person. All of this raises the possibility that wishes for assistance in suicide might predictably be granted to people who lack decisional capacity—a prospect any humane society should view with concern. But concern should also be tempered by realism about our resources for beneficence and the likely imminence of death. It is true that the possibility of new treatments or "miraculous" remissions and so on must not be overlooked even in near-death circumstances. But neither ought we institutionalize and impose irrational hope on that basis.

Question 1c: How can depression (as an example) be relevant to capacity to engage in assisted suicide?

Depression can, but need not, be accompanied by delusions. Beyond this, the connection(s) of depression with understanding and appreciation are not obvious and have been denied.[14] The word "depression" both describes a pattern of behavior and is used to refer to the cause(s) of that pattern. As a causal influence, depression can be identified as lying behind mood and, more contentiously perhaps, as the source of certain desires.

The terms "appreciation" and "understanding," while ordinary terms, are nonetheless logically complex and subtle. Both presuppose as a condition of application that a person is largely rational and has a largely consistent set of beliefs and desires. A general failure to meet these conditions renders a person unintelligible and makes it not feasible to attribute thoughts and so forth in explaining behavior. Depression can darken a person's mood. But a person of dark mood is not necessarily thereby unable to resist the mood, nor unable to understand and appreciate all sorts of choices. Depression becomes suspect vis à vis mental competence when certain desires seem overwhelmingly strong *and* out of normal character. But "overwhelmingly strong" is a problematic phrase. One thing it can mean is that certain desires (e.g., desires to die) are not well supported by reasons, or amenable to change in light of them, especially reasons that distinguish alternatives as preferable in the wider context of a person's beliefs, desires and other attitudes.

The susceptibility of desires to reason seems to us implied in the concept of appreciation.[15] If one cannot adjust one's actions (all things considered) in accord with one's reasoned preferences, one cannot act as one values. And if one cannot reason about one's preferences in light of available evidence, then can one be said to appreciate the alternatives? Clearly, not every desire or preference is immediately within rational control in the sense that if "unwanted" it simply vanishes. But we can sometimes identify a person as *in the grip* of forces beyond his control, foreign to his usual character, and for which (perhaps) he is not responsible.[16] Attribution of such forces is justified when it explains a person's behavior better than any alternative explanation (especially an alternative that exhibits the behavior as rational).

Which hypothesis/explanation best explains behavior can be a complex and contentious matter. It probably leaves room for a certain degree of indeterminacy that can be relevant morally as well: when it is indeterminate which of two competing explanations best explains a person's behavior, and each would lead to different judgments regarding decisional capacity, it would seem unethical to select the one such explanatory story that would lead to the removal of civil liberties. It can be difficult, of course, to tell whether two theories are genuinely equal in accounting for the evidence. It may be to expect too much to ask of mortal assessors that they put forward possible explanations/interpretations and simultaneously remain dispassionately neutral regarding their merits.[17] As with the criminal law, on the other hand, it is also often clear enough to most which account best explains a situation after all the arguments are in.[18]

Construed as a general proposal, the above quote from Peruzzi et al. about controlling depression or judging it incurable could serve to complicate matters. Treatment for depression may not be desired, hence capacity to consent to treatment could become an issue as well. Consent to treatment will tend to arise as an issue in cases where depression (or some other distorting influence or disorder)[19] is thought to be present and 1) treatment is undesired and 2) depression may compromise decisional capacity. Of course, treatment will be justified only if it is likely to benefit the person. Indeed, it is possible to envision tragic cases where, for example, we can make a good case that the desire to die is caused by depression and capacity is lacking, but a refusal of treatment would be competent. In the more usual case what will need guarding against is the tendency to assume that mere diagnosis of depression settles questions of capacity and treatment or obviates the need for detailed justification of a judgment regarding capacity.

Question 1d: Who should assess decisional capacity regarding assisted suicide? And 1e: Is there reason to believe mental health professionals in particular will "get it right"?

Given the subtleties already discussed regarding factors such as risk and depression there is reason to wonder whether they will generally be appreciated in practice. Indeed, no one profession would seem to have special expertise with regard to competence. Rather, competence lies in a complex territory at the intersection of law, philosophy (due to the concepts of "understanding," "appreciation" and "rationality"), the mental health professions and much "common sense." Our point is that no particular discipline focuses on issues peculiar to this area. We do not claim that no one person can possess enough relevant knowledge to assess capacity reliably. Following the frequently tried (and sometimes true) strategy of specialization, we could develop a new discipline of capacity assessment, or some current discipline could embrace it as a subspecialty. At present, however, there is reason to be concerned about the quality of capacity assessments. Courts, multidisciplinary panel systems or even public tribunals akin to juries may be preferable to reliance on current professions (provided special expertise is available when relevant). It is a legitimate worry as to whether current laws work better in theory than practice[20] (at least in "hard" cases). If one factors in concern about the ways in which professions can behave self-interestedly and tend to exhibit atypical value systems in certain ways,[21] it is clear that professionals may subtly influence patient choices through expression of their own values and never quite attain universal "best practices." If there are professional tendencies to rely overly on inferences from diagnostic category to competency status or disciplinary tendencies to pathologize unduly—matters about which one encounters heated assertions more than good research—then the worries deepen.[22] Many of these concerns, of course, are generic; while bearing on capacity to decide regarding suicide, they seem to raise few new or special worries here.

Question 2: Is there a specific capacity to decide regarding assisted suicide?

We have so far finessed the question of precisely *what* decisional capacity is/would be at issue in cases of assisted suicide and what criteria would plausibly define that capacity. Today, decisional capacities are treated as distinguishable into discrete functional areas (e.g., capacity to make financial decisions, testamentary capacity, capacity to decide regarding specific treatments, etc.). This means that capacity assessments have to be more refined than was true when global conceptions of capacity held sway.

There may be an inclination to assimilate the relevant capacity within capacity to decide treatment. But there are good reasons to resist such an assimilation. Treatments generally are intended to benefit a sick person by removing or ameliorating a condition that harms or limits the person. (Painkillers occupy an awkward position in this regard, since they often modify the person's experience rather than the underlying condition more directly.) These specific goals of treatment have been cited as distinguishing medicine and medical issues from wider concerns about well-being.[23] Aid in committing suicide bypasses this focus on underlying condition, which worries many who oppose assisted suicide or medical/health care involvement in it.[24] Treatments are frequently proposed by health care providers giving rise to concern that allowing health care providers to propose suicide opens the door to undue influence and coercion. For these reasons, it is better not to assume that capacity to request assisted suicide is a form of capacity to consent to treatment. Instead, we should attempt to define the capacity in question.

What should a person contemplating assisted suicide understand and appreciate to have decisional capacity? Despite individual and cultural variances about death most, if not all, will agree that death means the cessation of activity and experience in this world.[25] Beyond that, people may hold other convictions (survival, extinction, eternal bliss, damnation, reincarnation, etc.). No defensible public policy in a liberal democracy should take sides on the latter.

A plausible set of criteria defining the capacity in question might be: 1) The person knows he/she suffers from a terminal or chronic illness; 2) The person is able to understand generally what death is, and able to appreciate that certain actions, which are to be specified in advance and understood by the person, will lead to irreversible loss of agency and experience in this world for him/her. (Additional operational criteria that go beyond the definition of this capacity might be required, for example, the person desires to die;[26] the person desires aid in bringing about a death acceptable to him or her.[27]) This is a low standard of understanding, nor should it be high if part of the goal is to facilitate relief for those suffering acutely. Even so, not everyone will achieve it, so it may be defensible as establishing a genuine decisional capacity (though we offer no extended defense here).

Question 3: How much does the presence or absence of decisional capacity settle? In particular, should we ever honor incompetent requests for assisted suicide?

We will assume that the presence of the capacity to decide regarding assisted suicide, once enshrined in law, would rule out interference from the state (provided due process is followed). Whether or not this creates any positive duty to assist should also be clarified in law. It is widely assumed no such duty would arise, thereby leaving whomever the law would allow to assist as free to do so or not in accord with their conscience.

But what of the "other side" of the matter? It frequently happens that a person found incapable in a certain realm of decision making can still articulate tolerably clear preferences. The status of such preferences remains unclear legally and morally, as well as sometimes conceptually.[28] Could a person desire to die, desire assistance in achieving that end, yet fail to pass the criteria listed above? If so, are there circumstances under which we should honor such desires? The desire to die will generally be less clear to the degree that the person fails to meet the criteria we outlined, for example. Odd, confused or delusional beliefs about death might make it quite dubious that a person has the ability to understand or appreciate enough to decide. Yet, it may be tolerably clear that the person desires *to die*.[29]

Discussion of decision making for incompetent persons has focused upon whether a "best interests" standard should guide surrogate decision makers, or some version of "substituted judgment." For the sort of decisions under discussion, to decide whether death is in a person's best interests is to decide the value, to that person, of continued life. The *Latimer* case and others like it make plain how poignant and difficult such decisions can be—and also how unavoidable. Cases where a person desires to die but lacks decisional capacity sharpen the unclear status of incompetent persons by raising the possibility that life might be *imposed* on someone against her will. Is the simple wish to die against the person's best interests? Circumstances can make that rather unclear. At the very least, the presence of a clearly expressed wish to die will add to the discomfort level of surrogates/guardians. It will also tend to put pressure on findings of incapacity to be justified in detail because the acute suffering is then being *imposed* by further treatment or care.

When the request for assisted suicide stems from extreme terminal suffering, the obligation to relieve suffering seems sufficient to justify providing assistance. Where death is not imminent but suffering is present and experienced or judged as unbearable, we have to judge the quality of another's life in ways that involve the unavoidable limits of our own capacity to be moved by another's plight.[30] Observers will be influenced by their own history or experience of suffering, their religious beliefs, their ability to empathize with and understand the lives of others and so forth. All these and more are present in any judgment about the quality of life of another.

The very possibility of incompetent wishes for assistance in dying may undermine the sense (in certain quarters) that assisted suicide might be morally and procedurally clearer than euthanasia. With assisted suicide, it is frequently thought, we can avoid issues of one person evaluating the quality of life of another. This may still be true in the vast majority of cases. Nevertheless, the wish to die (where it does not meet the test of competence) must be taken seriously when the person is suffering intently.

We have been discussing cases of incompetent wishes to die in the absence of advance directives. Such directives provide the clearest case where a surrogate decision maker could rely on the person's own prior and competent desires in deciding whether or not assisted suicide is right. Inference to what a person "would want" gets more dubious the farther it gets from what has been expressed quite explicitly. Unless one knows another's attitudes in great detail (and even then there are indeterminacies even the person herself cannot "know" in advance), there is lots of room for a person to surprise even intimates by drawing unexpected conclusions. Some[31] would have it that a surrogate decision maker is never justified in imposing an undesired option on a person lacking decisional capacity unless it can be shown that were the person competent they would desire the same course of action. While this would be *sufficient* to defend a course of action it is not necessary. Often determining what a person would want if competent is highly speculative (most obviously in cases of lifelong incompetence). Hence, we suggest that this standard places too high a burden on surrogate decision makers. Even when an advance directive is explicit, problems can arise associated with matters of interpretation, unforeseen possibilities and varying evaluations of suffering or quality of life.[32] Moreover, competent prior wishes for or against suicide can conflict with clear present wishes for the opposite. While it seems paradoxical even to consider having incompetent wishes outweighing competent ones, it also seems odd to consider assisting a person in *committing suicide* when he/she does not any longer wish to die.

We will not attempt to resolve these issues here. Instead we will content ourselves with a few observations: There is a tendency to see reflective or critical capacities and interests as essential not only to the possession of autonomy and the possession of decisional capacity, but also to the value of life, the status of personhood or personal identity.[33] Most adults possess such abilities in varying degrees. What is more, most of us see them as valuable or essential to our identity as shaped by our acts and choices. Respect for such capacities (and/or those who possess them) is one important motivation behind most attempts to liberalize our practices of caring for the dying. Even quite young children with little of such capacities nonetheless look forward to the day when they are granted the liberty accompanying such capacities. On the other hand, all of us grew into possession of such capacities gradually, and we will likely face a gradual loss of them with aging. There are people who live their whole lives with compromised or no such capacities. Therefore, two distinct concerns arise: 1) relevance to issues of decisional authority; 2) relevance to the obligations of others toward the diminished. It can be threatening to speak of "diminished persons" and the like. When such talk is clearly restricted to the first concern it may be less offensive. But 1) and 2) are not obviously separable or independent issues. It may be that emphasis on advance directives as expressing the autonomous will of competent person reflects or encourages the thought that it is the conditions necessary for 1) which lie at the heart of the value of human life, hence which sustain 2). However that may be, liberalization proposals regarding assisted suicide will benefit in both clarity and acceptability to many to the extent they address clearly the issue of incompetent wishes as it links up with such general concerns of value.

A semantic approach to the issue of assisted suicide could help clarify matters if it treated assisted *suicide* as relevant only where decisional capacity exists. Such a solution might have advantages in making plainer that it is a surrogate's decision ultimately in such cases, and not the incompetent person's irrespective of whatever incompetent wishes may be expressed. This "solution" would, of course, also require a clearly applicable standard—"best interests" or some other—to guide decision makers when capacity is lacking. On the other hand, such a policy might lead surrogates to undervalue or even not consider the desires of the incompetent person—an effect some claim to have noted in the practice of guardianship.[34] At present, the moral problem of how to account for incompetent desires remains unsolved: the law has not explicitly said what is to be done in such cases.[35]

Conclusion

The issues we have raised lie very much at the margins of any actual policy regarding assisted suicide. There may be a tendency to think that since these issues will affect rather few cases (as a percentage of the total), they don't merit the focus of attention. Yet we must explore such issues to be morally responsible in formulating actual, workable policies because the needed distinctions and clear limits are necessary to liberalize our laws and practices around death and dying. A failure to do so exposes us to various forms of potential error and may lead to a slide down the "slippery slope." Debate can be general; implementation must be specific.

1. Peruzzi, Canapary and Bongar, 1996: 359.

2. Madigan, Checkland and Silberfeld, 1994.

3. Battin, 1982a; Prado, 1998.

4. We are not here ruling out a general policy of insisting on a capacity evaluation prior to any provision of assistance in committing suicide. One basis for such a policy, however, is likely to be the protection of those assisting against charges of murder, coercion or lack of due care. These sorts of reasons are not the focus of the current paragraph so much as beneficent concern for the person requesting assistance.

5. See Silberfeld and Fish, 1994: 109–120; Silberfeld, 1992; Pepper-Smith et al., 1992.

6. In the case of a will the "risk" involved is not so much to the person as that her will might be frustrated, hence assessment is warranted *if desired*. Here, though, the desire for an assessment is rather more the reason than risk. Assessment may also be justified by a need to clarify the interests of *others* involved.

7. "Risk" involves both the degree of likelihood that a particular evil may befall one—approaching 100 percent in the case of the terminally ill—and the nature of the hazard incurred.

8. We are here assuming that the vast majority of requests for assisted suicide will be from those who are either terminally ill and suffering, or are chronically ill or disabled and suffering. Cases of persons who are no longer up to, in Cole Porter's phrase, "fighting bravely that old ennui" raise different ethical issues since the sole basis for second-party involvement would be respect for another's autonomy. While that can generate a negative right to non-interference, it is far less clear that it generates any obligation to help (see Battin, 1994: 107–113).

9. See Drane, 1985; Wilks, 1997.

10. See Checkland and Silberfeld, 1996.

11. In another paper we have argued that often this will necessitate an assessor making and defending singular causal judgments about various influences on a person—judgments supported, perhaps, by experience, but lacking the backing of anything close to general laws (Silberfeld and Checkland, 1999). This means that, in hard cases, judgments of capacity will be inherently contestable, not because there is no right answer, but because the "right" or "best" answer will involve a complex amalgam of singular causal claims (often backed by specialized knowledge), general inductive knowledge, sophisticated interpretation of a person's attitudes (beliefs, desires, intentions, dispositions, etc.) and other lore.

12. Data on depression in the terminally ill is scant. Silverstone et al. (1996) discuss the prevalence of major depressive disorder in medical in-patients more generally, finding approximately 10 percent of in-patients suffering therefrom. Other studies have placed estimates higher or lower, and methodological issues abound. A recurrent theme in the literature is the difficulties faced in accurate diagnosis of depression in the physically ill.

13. Peruzzi, Canapay and Bongar, 1996: 360.

14. Culver and Gert, 1990: 624ff.

15. Checkland and Silberfeld, 1996; Silberfeld and Checkland, 1999.

16. The point of the last condition is to suggest that we may have quite different attitudes to cases of "uncontrollable" anger than toward depression precisely because we recognize/impose a norm on all adults to develop their characters in ways that enables them to control their anger in certain ways *no matter what*. This also brings out how talk merely of the *strength* of desires can mislead; people typically have desires of different orders, and higher/reflective desires must generally (but not perfectly) accord with lower or more basic desires (see Hurley, 1989). Clearly, more needs to be said about such matters, but if there is a norm akin to that we suggest, anger could never render one incompetent (though we might mitigate liability under extreme provocation or lack of opportunity to develop appropriate reflective capacities). Fear and other emotions need to treated individually. In adding responsibility to the list of considerations we are not supposing that it is in general possible to determine who is capable of responsibility prior to determination of capacity (see Elliot, 1991).

17. Such cases, among others, point out the need for adequate and sophisticated appeal procedures.

18. A further issue we skirt here is the appropriate standard of evidence in capacity assessment—"beyond reasonable doubt," "balance of probabilities" or some other.

19.   We are discussing depression because it is likely to come up in many cases and its relevance to capacity has been misrepresented (we think). But it is only one possible mental disorder or "external" cause that might be relevant to assessment of capacity. The nature of any relevance needs to be thought through in each case and for each disorder.

20.   David Guifridda has put the issue rather provocatively as follows: "If it only works in theory and not practice, does it even work in theory?"

21.   Veatch, 1995: 75.

22.   Maltsberger (1994) has argued that the link between suicide and depression has been exaggerated "because suicidal thinking or behavior are among the criteria" for diagnosing depression (Peruzzi, Canapary and Bongar, 1996). This may be so. Logically, however, there is no circularity provided suicidal ideation alone does not settle the question of depression.

23.   Callahan, 1995.

24.   For example, Gaylin et al., 1988.

25.   Some may deny this, believing that the dead "watch over" and influence our lives. In such cases, the difference death makes to experience and agency would be the appropriate locus of investigation. At one extreme, a person who sees death as making *no* difference fails to appreciate something. Milder views will have less clear implications. Could we say that a person should understand that what happens after death is unknown? Clearly that is not only contentious, i.e., some will believe they know damn well what happens (including cessation of experience as one possibility under "what happens"), but more importantly, some people will consider maintenance on their part of particular views as morally significant ("The faithful shall be saved") in ways a public policy about assisted suicide should be sensitive to. Enabling legislation would probably need to say something about such complexities, but the question of adequate wording we will sidestep here.

26.   The Dutch criterion that such a desire be "enduring" aims at testing for the authenticity or "all things considered" nature of the desire to die. Clearly, this is important since we want to avoid rushing to the "aid" of anyone who blurts out such desires when depressed, suffering or under pathological influence, which makes the desire's authenticity suspect. Any legal reform might want to specify such matters in statute.

27.   We assume that "acceptability" will usually involve matters of timing, the presence of others and degree of suffering involved. Weird cases where a person wants to die in a ritual manner might require resources beyond capacity-assessment to deal with.

28.   Silberfeld and Fish, 1994.

29.   In cases of compromised ability to consider alternatives due to depression, a person may understand what assisted suicide would do, but fail to appreciate the alternatives, hence lack decisional ability.

30.   Limits can be set to the role we accord sympathy when the person suffering is competent, but it cannot be eliminated even there. And clearly its role expands when one must decide for another. Regarding such limits, see Battin (1994: 111): "That someone voluntarily and knowingly requests release from what he or she experiences as misery is sufficient, other things being equal, for the request to be honored...we cannot insist on independent, objective evidence that mercy would in fact be served, or that death is better than pain. We can

demand such evidence to protect a perfectly healthy person, and we can summon it to end the sufferings of someone who can no longer choose; but we cannot demand it or use it for the seriously ill person."

31. For example, Gustafson, 1993.

32. See Dworkin, 1993; Dresser, 1995.

33. For example, Dworkin, 1993.

34. A number of advocacy groups have argued that the institutions of guardianship/surrogate decision makers have this general tendency to diminish the importance and relevance of the residual capacity possessed by those found incompetent. Some groups have advocated for the elimination of guardianship, especially when applied to the intellectually disabled, offering various forms of "supported" decision making instead. We assume for present purposes the continued existence of guardianship and ask instead, "How should a guardian give appropriate weight to the preferences of an incompetent ward?"

35. Silberfeld and Fish, 1994; Dresser, 1994.

Bronwyn Singleton

THE MEDIA PERSPECTIVE[1]

This annotated bibliography provides a substantial sampling of media coverage surrounding the issue of assisted suicide. The articles cover a span of 11 years (1988–1999), but the selection is weighted toward the last four (1996–1999). In order to make the project more manageable this bibliography focuses on coverage of assisted suicide, euthanasia and related issues in three national newspapers. From July 1989 to April 1999 we collected articles from *The Globe and Mail*. In October 1998 the *National Post* was introduced. Due to considerations to do with editorial policy and extent of coverage, we began collecting articles from the *National Post* in preference to *The Globe and Mail*, although there is overlap in the coverage for some months.

In addition to articles from Canadian newspapers, we judged it necessary to include articles from a U.S. newspaper because of the impact of developments in the U.S.—especially the 1997 Supreme Court decision—on Canadian public opinion and precedent law. Extent of coverage, editorial policy and circulation were the major factors for choosing *The New York Times* as the *de facto* national newspaper in the United States. It is also the case that many of the stories carried in *The Globe and Mail* were taken from *The New York Times*.

These articles, then, offer a primarily North American perspective on assisted suicide and related issues, although there

---

is noticeable interest shown in how the debate advances in other parts of the world, particularly in the Netherlands and Australia.

Despite the disparate tenors of individual articles, overall the press has provided remarkably balanced coverage of this debate. Much of the reporting is surprisingly neutral considering the controversial and emotional nature of the topic. When more impassioned views are given voice, there is usually an effort made to allow both supporters and detractors of assisted suicide to be heard.

Several themes emerge in these articles. Dr. Jack Kevorkian figures prominently in the ongoing debates, despite, or perhaps because of, what seems to be increasing public uncertainty about his tactics. Dr. Timothy Quill is also referred to repeatedly, although in contrast to Kevorkian, Quill's activities are consistently represented in a positive light. Canadian legal cases involving Robert Latimer and Dr. Nancy Morrison receive considerable coverage in *The Globe and Mail*, while United States Supreme Court rulings on constitutional issues associated with assisted suicide and the attenuating fallout, particularly in the state of Oregon, are attentively reported in the American and, to a somewhat lesser extent, Canadian press. Concerns regarding an aging population, advancing medical technology and intensifying economic demands on an increasingly encumbered social "safety net," as well as questions about cultural treatment of death and dying, all figure in ongoing discussion and debate relating to assisted suicide.

National Post Articles

1999

May 24. "'Professor Death' facing protests." (Anon.)

Article reports on the controversy surrounding the appointment of Peter Singer at Princeton University, due to his views on killing disabled babies with a goal to eliminate suffering in the world, which some claim are indications of his bigotry against people with disabilities.

May 21. "Man to go home, ending do-not-resuscitate debate."
(Adrian Humphreys)

Article reports on the improving health of a 79-year-old man
who was the subject of a court battle between his wife and
Riverview Health Centre after Mrs. Sawatzky noticed that the
hospital had placed a do-not-resuscitate order on her husband
Mr. Sawatzky's chart without consulting her.

May 6. "Top court announces today whether it will hear Latimer appeal." (Adam Killick)

Article reports on Robert Latimer awaiting the decision of
Saskatchewan's Supreme Court on whether or not to hear his
appeal on a life sentence for killing his severely disabled daughter in 1997.

May 2. "Doctors fall prey to assisted-suicide copycat effect:
Study." (Adrian Humphreys)

Article reports on a phenomenon called the "copycat effect,"
which describes the effects that publicized cases of assisted suicides have on similar cases with a reported increase in deaths in
the month following the publicized case.

May 1. "Suicide's bitter legacy." (Elizabeth Schaal)

Author writes about an Ottawa woman whose lover killed himself and the effects this has had on her life and claims that our
society has romanticized suicide resulting in a greater acceptance, especially of assisted suicide for terminally ill patients.

April 21. "Dr. Death's dark vision and the value of life." (Nor-
man Doidge)

Author gives reasons for the increasing attention surrounding
euthanasia even after Dr. Kevorkian's sentencing. He also speculates on the consequences of legalizing euthanasia for depressed persons and suggests that those doctors who are most
reluctant to perform assisted suicides should be the ones to perform it.

April 15. Cartoon caption. (G. Clement)

A caption reading "Suddenly Dr. Kevorkian felt overwhelmingly...homesick" under a caricature of a prison guard leading Dr.
Kevorkian to his cell and passing a "Lethal Injection Chamber."

April 15. "Kevorkian has the right to starve in Michigan prison." (Anon.)

Article reports that Kevorkian's lawyer maintains that a new jail policy recently passed preventing prisoners from being force-fed is a reaction to Dr. Kevorkian's plan to starve himself, although Michigan prison officials claim otherwise.

April 14. "'Dr. Death' faces up to 25 years for mercy killing." (Charles Laurence)

Article reports the reactions of the "Not Dead Yet" movement to Dr. Kevorkian's "stiff sentence." Kevorkian sentenced to 10 to 25 years in prison for second-degree murder and also reprimanded for breaking the law and using the court to further political goals. Kevorkian's lawyers plan to appeal.

April 11. "Morrison receives support from fellow Nova Scotia doctors." (Gloria Galloway)

Article reports on various Nova Scotia physicians supporting Dr. Morrison, claiming that her actions were not deviant, and disagreeing with the College of Physicians and Surgeons of Nova Scotia's decision to issue a formal reprimand that will be kept permanently in Dr. Morrison's records.

April 11. "Choose death." (O. G. Pamp, Editorial)

Editorial reacting to a March 27, 1999 article vilifying Dr. Kevorkian as a "medical hitman." Author considers the choice to die an issue of individual freedom.

April 5. "Murder most inappropriate." (Andrew Coyne)

Author reviews and reconsiders the Hippocratic Oath in light of Dr. Morrison's recent case dismissal. The author claims that although Dr. Morrison has been reprimanded, she has breached the Oath and the law and yet remains free to practice medicine.

March 31. "'Remorseful' doctor admits hastening death was wrong." (Gloria Galloway)

Article reviews Dr. Nancy Morrison's act of mercy killing a cancer patient, which led to a subsequently dropped murder charge. Dr. Morrison accepted a reprimand from the College of Physicians and Surgeons of Nova Scotia, acknowledging she was wrong to hasten her patient's death.

March 30. "Ending the killing ground of euthanasia." (Mark Pickup)

Author claims that the recent second-degree murder conviction of Dr. Kevorkian indicates to the disabled, "unattractive, unwanted, broken people of America (and Canada)" that they are valuable and that lawful acceptance of the right to die would inevitably translate into a duty to die.

March 30. "The right to die; not to murder." (Susan Martinuk)

Author reviews Kevorkian's history starting with the early classified ad offering to assist in suicides that led to his first patient. Author comments that Kevorkian's recent conviction indicates that society is not ready to grant physicians the right to kill and that only the "misguided" buy into "the kook" Kevorkian's philosophy.

March 30. "Death expert Kübler-Ross reaches stage five." (Brad Evenson)

Article reports on Dr. Kübler-Ross' book *On Death and Dying* and her five stages of death. Discusses how Kübler-Ross claims to herself have reached the fifth stage and is ready to die while addressing corollary criticisms levied against Kübler-Ross for "over-standardizing" death.

March 27. "Medical hit man's mission stopped." (Charles Laurence)

Author briefly reviews Kevorkian's history of assisted suicides leading to Thomas Youk's active euthanasia and his earlier "medical" writing. Also discusses the views of some of Kevorkian's supporters who nevertheless think Kevorkian has gone too far and has destroyed his own cause by grandstanding.

March 27. "Kevorkian guilty of murder for 'mercy' killing." (Charles Laurence)

Article reports the guilty verdict in Kevorkian's trial for second-degree murder and delivery of a controlled substance, Kevorkian having been released with a promise of no more assisted suicides until his sentence hearing on April 14.

March 26. "Kevorkian's 'final solution' in jury's hands." (Charles Laurence)

Kevorkian jury remains out while deliberating on the fate of Kevorkian and the euthanasia debate. Article reviews the final day of trial in which Kevorkian asked the jury to grant him the right to administer the "final solution," which prosecutors claim is too similar to Hitler's "final solution."

March 24. "Kevorkian prosecution rests case—quickly." (Charles Laurence)

Article reports on the progress of the Kevorkian trial, which looks grim after a ruling by Judge Cooper disallows the jury from hearing how Kevorkian killed Thomas Youk. This decision comes after prosecution dropped charges of assisted suicide that would have allowed emotional testimony from the family and evidence of Youk's suffering.

March 23. "Kevorkian says his actions are excusable homicide." (Anon.)

Article briefly outlines the steps leading to Kevorkian's charge of first-degree murder and reports on the first day of the trial in which Kevorkian is representing himself, claiming that his actions should be considered "excusable homicide" like the actions of executioners or soldiers.

March 22. "Did Kevorkian go too far this time?" (Charles Laurence)

Author reports that what prosecutors claim is murder, Kevorkian maintains is active euthanasia and no different from assisted suicide, for which he had been acquitted four times earlier. Author also reports on an interview with Kevorkian and depicts him as a cold, ruthless man with a fetish for death.

March 16. "Dying woman's euthanasia TV ad to be broadcast." (Michael Perry)

Article reports on the Australian decision to allow a dying woman to air a TV ad asking for the right to die despite the protests of anti-euthanasia groups who argue the ad will only encourage suicides for everyone and not only patients who are terminally ill.

February 10. "Family disputes doctor's treatment of dying father." (Lynn Moore)

Article reports on day two of an inquest into the death of a 76-year-old man taken off a respirator against his wishes and the wishes of the family. The patient's son claims doctors were continually pressuring for his consent to take his father off the respirator once they learned that his father's medical situation was irreversible.

February 9. "Do-not-resuscitate order put on medical record 3 weeks before patient's death, inquiry told." (Lynn Moore)

Article reports on an inquiry into the death of a 76-year-old man after a do-not-resuscitate order was placed on the patient's medical record against the wishes of his family. Doctors argue the family was consulted.

January 29. "Foolish suicide, not mercy killing." (Joseph Couture)

Author writes of the pressures an able-bodied woman in her 80s receives from right-to-die activists to end her life even though her pleas seem, to the author, more like cries for attention and release from the promise of a lonely life.

January 13. "Understanding death from a patient's perspective." (Brad Evenson)

Article reporting on a study with terminally ill patients commenting on quality end-of-life care, concluding that patients need to "receive adequate pain and symptom management, avoid inappropriate prolongation of dying, achieve a sense of control, relieve burden and strengthen relationships with loved ones."

January 11. "Life and death." (Peter Lawson, Brian Quinn, Editorials)

Two editorials responding to January 6 commentary "Do you sincerely want me to live?," one condemning the author for lack of sympathy for those who want to "die with dignity" and the second equating euthanasia with Hitler's cleansing of those who were deemed "unnecessary burdens."

January 8. "Life and death." (Mel Graham, Editorial)

Editorial responding to January 6 commentary "Do you sincerely want me to live?" supporting author's concern about the rise of euthanasia in Canada.

January 8. "Man, 80, to be tried on charge he aided ailing wife's suicide." (Adam Killick)

Article reports on an 80-year-old man being accused of assisting in his wife's suicide due to her excruciating pain. She is reported as saying that her decision to end her life is different from those decisions made by a third party for persons who are not mentally sound.

January 6. "Do you sincerely want me to live?" (Mark Pickup)

An emotional commentary by a man who has chronic, progressive multiple sclerosis stating that the existence of euthanasia indicates that the disabled are held in low regard and that there are arbitrary and objective standards that outline which lives are not worthy to live.

January 2. "Hellish choices." (N. B. Hershfield, Editorial)

Editorial in response to November 23 commentary "Who decides when care is futile?" points out that the author does not consider quality of life for terminally ill patients.

1998

December 12. "A TV program to die for." (Mark Steyn)

Author casts an unfavorable light on *60 Minutes* for airing Dr. Kevorkian's assisted suicide and through a review of his past depicts Kevorkian as a man fascinated with death. Author claims that euthanasia is "killing for convenience at the end of life" as abortion is "killing for convenience at the beginning of life."

December 12. "Nova Scotia decides to end Morrison prosecution." (Graeme Hamilton)

Author reports on Nova Scotia prosecutor's decision not to appeal a Supreme Court ruling to release Dr. Nancy Morrison from first-degree murder charges, but also reports on the possibility that the College of Physicians and Surgeons may take disciplinary action.

December 12. "Lights, camera, death." (Mark Steyn)

Motivated by the broadcast of Dr. Kevorkian injecting Tom Youk with a lethal dose of drugs, the author offers a very opinionated look at what he calls "convenience killings" in the form of euthanasia, assisted suicide and abortion.

December 10. "Kevorkian to stand trial." (Anon.)

Article reports on judge's decision to have Dr. Kevorkian stand trial for first-degree murder, which could lead to sentence of life in prison.

December 2. "Law and order." (Bronwyn Eyre, Gale White, R. W. Krutzen, Editorials)

One editorial responding to November 25 article "Speaking for the victims" and clarifying legal points of fact to support Latimer's original verdict. Two further editorials responding to November 28 article "No suffering in Robert Latimer," one of which supports author's description of Latimer's daughter, Tracy, being treated like a farm animal and the other which disagrees with this.

November 28. "No suffering in Robert Latimer." (Christie Blatchford)

Author comments on the similarities of Robert Latimer's killing his disabled daughter, Tracy, and pig farmers killing their pigs when they cannot feed them, and condemns Latimer for "callously" applying the "law of the farm" to his child.

November 26. "Life expectancy outpacing nations' health care." (Araminta Wordsworth)

Article outlines two recent reports indicating a longer life expectancy around the world and raises concerns regarding care of the elderly by quoting a doctor as saying, "We'd rather kill people than deal with them."

November 26. "Kevorkian charged with murder." (Michael Ellis)

Author reports on the prosecutor's decision to charge Dr. Kevorkian with first-degree murder, criminal assistance of a suicide and delivery of a controlled substance.

November 25. "Speaking for the victims." (Andrew Coyne)

Author comments on the Latimer sentence and outlines reasons why mercy killing is objectionable, citing the Sawatzky case where doctors imposed a do-not-resuscitate order against the wishes of the family.

November 24. "TV death looks like murder: Prosecutor." (Michael Ellis)

Article reports that prosecutors are being careful not to bring a premature murder charge against Dr. Kevorkian and are viewing the videotaped death of Thomas Youk. Argues that Youk's death was staged to fulfill Kevorkian's "attention starved ego."

November 24. "Journey continues for Latimer family." (Elena Cherney)

Article reviews the steps leading to Latimer's 10-year sentence and reports on the family's hope that Latimer's case will be heard in Supreme Court followed with a release from his sentence.

November 24. "Court says Latimer must serve 10 years." (Francine Dubé)

Article reports on Robert Latimer's 10-year sentence for ending his severely disabled daughter's life, after an original sentence of two years less a day was appealed. This original sentence angered those activists who believe that persons with disabilities lead meaningful lives.

November 23. "Who decides when care is futile?" (Wesley J. Smith)

Author claims do-not-resuscitate orders against the wishes of the family are "legalized murder." Author comments on cases where patients do not want to die despite advice of doctors who claim that care is futile or inappropriate.

November 23. "Dr. Death's latest public spectacle may have injured his own cause." (Marina Jimenez)

Author claims that despite Dr. Kevorkian's claims, the right to die should also be extended to those who cannot do it for themselves. Argues that the Thomas Youk video showing Kevorkian administering a lethal injection to Youk has hurt the doctor-assisted suicide cause more than it has helped it.

November 23. "On international TV, Kevorkian kills a man." (Dan Westell)

Article reports on *60 Minutes* featuring Thomas Youk's Kevorkian-assisted suicide. Kevorkian released video coverage of the event in hopes of forcing authorities to charge him so that he may draw attention to the issue of assisted suicide and test the rights of terminally ill patients.

October 28. "Compassion is no defense: Crown attorney." (Graeme Hamilton)

Author reports on a Supreme Court judge's decision to support a provincial court ruling that the Dr. Nancy Morrison manslaughter case be discharged, despite the Crown attorney's appeal to reopen the case.

October 28. "For whom the bell tolls." (Judith Snow)

A severely disabled woman gives her perspective on the issue of assisted suicide. The author attempts to show how the life of a disabled person may still be desirable, and expresses her belief that only each person him/herself can decide such a course of action.

The Globe and Mail Articles

(Note that particularly in 1995, 1996 and 1997, a good
number of articles on assisted suicide appearing in
The Globe and Mail were reprinted from *The New York Times*.)

1999

April 28. "MD's sentence upheld." (Lila Sarick)

Article reports that Maurice Généreux's sentence of two years
less a day in a provincial reformatory was upheld by the Ontario
Court of Appeal.

April 17. "Kevorkian's courage." (K. F. Muething)

Writer condemns Judge Cooper for her harsh sentence of
Dr. Jack Kevorkian, and praises Kevorkian for his courage.

April 14. "Kevorkian jailed 10 to 25 years: Judge lectures suicide doctor who flouted law." (Dirk Johnson)

Article reports that Kevorkian has been sentenced to 10 to 25
years in prison by Judge Jessica Cooper, and documents Cooper's condemnation of Kevorkian's violation of the law, as well
as the various reactions to the sentence.

April 3. "Safe morphine levels." (Dana MacDonald)

Author is prompted by comments made in the following article
to explain that, due to the development of tolerance, increases in
doses of morphine are often necessary to maintain the same
pain relief, and that small, slow increases do not put a patient at
risk.

March 31. "Doctor accepts reprimand over death of patient;
Morrison admits she erred in giving injection that hastened man's demise." (Alison Auld)

Article reports on Dr. Nancy Morrison's signing of a letter draft-
ed by the Nova Scotia College of Physicians and Surgeons acknowledging that she was wrong to hasten her patient's death.

March 27. "Kevorkian convicted of murder: Doctor videotaped lethal injection." (Anon.)

Article reports that Dr. Jack Kevorkian has been convicted of
second-degree murder, but has not yet been sentenced. Article
also reviews the details of the case and the trial.

March 26. "Kevorkian urges acquittal." (Anon.)

Article reports briefly on some of the tactics used by Kevorkian in his closing arguments.

March 24. "Kevorkian can't call widow as witness: Wife of man given lethal injection not allowed to testify before jury, judge rules." (Anon.)

Article documents the proceedings of Kevorkian's murder trial, including the problems he has faced in representing himself, the details of his defense and the specific events captured on the videotape that was shown on *60 Minutes*.

March 23. "Kevorkian defends himself at murder trial: Doctor argues he acted out of professional duty in videotaped administering of fatal injection." (Justin Hyde)

Article documents the details of Dr. Jack Kevorkian's trial on murder charges; the murder charges stem from a videotape that shows Kevorkian administering a lethal injection to a patient, which was shown on *60 Minutes*. Article also reports on Kevorkian's struggle to be able to represent himself, as well as his main line of defense, which involves the notion that as a physician, he has a duty to kill.

March 4. "A question of ethics: Tools for life; courses expanding at universities." (Wallace Immen)

Article reports that many Canadian universities are now including a course in ethics as part of business, law and medical programs. Article suggests that increased competitiveness of business, formalized codes of conduct in business and the publicity given to the business excesses of the 1980's are possible causes of this increase in ethics courses.

February 23. "Suicide and terminal illness." (Anon.)

Article reports on a study published in the *New England Journal of Medicine*, according to which the most common reason for using Oregon's new Death With Dignity Act cited by the 15 people who chose to do so in 1998 was a fear of loss of autonomy or control of bodily functions.

February 16. "Dutch MDs disregard euthanasia safeguards: Report says most cases unreported, unchecked." (Anon.)

Article reports on a survey published in the *Journal of Medical Ethics*, which shows that strict safeguards established by the

Royal Dutch Medical Association to control how and when euthanasia is performed are being ignored. It was found that almost two-thirds of cases of euthanasia and assisted suicide in 1995 were not reported, that in 20 percent of cases the patients did not explicitly request it, and that in 17 percent of cases other treatments were available.

February 4. "Saskatchewan: Latimer prosecutor let go." (Anon.)

Article reports that Randy Kirkham, the Saskatchewan prosecutor acquitted of obstructing justice in the Robert Latimer murder case, has lost his position with the provincial Justice Department for unspecified reasons.

January 15. "Passages." (Anon.)

Gerald Klooster has died of natural causes; Klooster was abducted by his own son in 1996, who wanted to prevent his mother from taking him to Dr. Jack Kevorkian.

January 11. "Latimer sentence too harsh, poll told: Tolerance shown for mercy killing." (Jeff Sallot)

Article documents a new poll, according to which 73 percent of Canadians feel Robert Latimer's mandatory life sentence for killing his disabled daughter is too harsh; it also reports that only 16 percent said mercy killing should be treated like any other murder.

January 9. "Lexicology: Measuring the public mood—in a word: From 'au pair' to 'paparazzi' to 'impeachment,' *Merriam-Webster's* online dictionary provides a see-through mirror for our collective consciousness." (Cullen Murphy)

Article reports that the *Merriam-Webster's Collegiate Dictionary* Website keeps a record of the most frequently looked-up words. After the *60 Minutes* broadcast showing footage of Dr. Jack Kevorkian administering a lethal injection to a terminally ill patient, the word "euthanasia" rose to No. 102 on that list.

January 6. "50 deaths investigated." (Anon.)

Article reports that about 50 deaths of patients in British hospitals are being investigated due to allegations of unsanctioned euthanasia.

1998

November 25. "CBS will hand over death tape." (Anon.)

CBS News agreed to hand over to police a videotape of Dr. Jack Kevorkian administering a lethal injection to the terminally ill Thomas Youk, 52; the tape will help prosecutors decide whether to charge Kevorkian.

November 24. "Televised euthanasia heats up U.S. debate: Kevorkian's mercy-killing on *60 Minutes* deliberately carried out as an act of defiance." (Paul Koring)

Article reports that Kevorkian's purpose in televising his act of euthanasia on CBS's *60 Minutes* was to heighten the debate over euthanasia in the United States. Also cites the various opinions of the family of those who Kevorkian has helped to die, the religious right, the Hemlock Society, the American Medical Association, as well as the results of opinion polls.

November 17. "Second opinion: Patient's beloved deserve a say." (Dr. Miriam Shuchman)

The author refers to the case of Andrew Sawatzky, arguing that even if his wife's wishes are not in his best interests, they should still be taken into account when a Do Not Resuscitate order is being considered, simply because she is his wife.

November 14. "The ethics of death spur intense debate: Who has the right to let a patient die? The experts aren't sure." (Sean Fine)

Reports the case of Andrew Sawatzky, in Winnipeg, whose wife objects to a Do Not Resuscitate order on his file; the order has been temporarily lifted. Criticizes the 1995 Joint Statement on Resuscitative Interventions for not specifying whether it is the family of the patient or the hospital who may make the final decision concerning a D.N.R. order by describing problematic cases and reporting conflicting expert opinions.

November 14. "Life and death: Court decides in wife's favor; judge orders Winnipeg hospital to lift Do Not Resuscitate order." (Sean Fine and David Roberts)

Describes the case of Andrew Sawatsky; a Do Not Resuscitate order, imposed by Winnipeg's Riverview Health Center, was temporarily lifted thanks to efforts from his wife, Helene. Reports Madam Justice Holly Beard's criticisms of the Public Trustee and of Riverview.

November 11. "A matter of simple justice." (Jeffrey Simpson)

Criticizes the House of Commons and the Chrétien government for not addressing the issues of euthanasia and assisted suicide in Canada, and blames their indifference for Dr. Nancy Morrison's reappearance in court. Charges that she assisted in the death of a cancer patient were dropped by a lower court judge, but she must now appear in Supreme Court.

October 17. "Human dignity: Who owns my life? Story of Sue Rodriguez raises life-and-death issues." (David Barber)

Article describes the made-for-TV movie *At the End of the Day: The Sue Rodriguez Story*, as well as the details and circumstances surrounding Rodriguez' court battle for an assisted suicide in the early 1990's.

October 17. "Medical advances stir interest in euthanasia: Some people feel a planned death is more appealing than prolonging the dying." (Jane Coutts)

Dr. Nuala Kenny, in her address to the World Medical Association, argued that legalizing euthanasia or assisted suicide would lead down a slippery slope. Her views are opposed with those of Dr. Rob Dillman, who cites the success of legalized euthanasia and assisted suicide in the Netherlands.

July 4. "Assisted suicide ban approved." (Anon.)

Michigan Legislature approved a ban making assisted suicide a crime punishable by up to five years in prison and a $10,000 fine.

July 3. "Doctor could face manslaughter charge: Nova Scotia attorney general wants clearer guidelines on when patients' lives can be terminated." (Murray Brewster)

Report on Nova Scotia's option to appeal a court decision to throw out charges against Dr. Nancy Morrison, charged with the death of a cancer patient, despite public support of the original dismissal. The article points to a need for legal clarification between crimes fueled by malicious or benign intentions. Intimates that Nova Scotia is using the appeal as a tactic to force the Canadian government to act on this issue.

July 1. "Vatican reins in theological dissent: No questioning permitted of 'definitive truths' such as ban on women priests; Pope takes aim at liberals." (Anon.)

Article reports on the apostolic letter issued by the Pope that declares deviations from Roman Catholicism's "definitive truths" to be a violation of church law. Some examples of such deviations include euthanasia, female priests and sex outside marriage.

June 6. "Reno sides with assisted-suicide law: U.S. Attorney-General's ruling protects MDs who help terminally ill patients die in Oregon." (Michael Sniffen)

Article documents the anti-assisted-suicide activities of Republican Henry Hyde, Democrat James Oberstar, President Bill Clinton, Lori Hougeens of the National Right to Life, Newt Gingrich and Drug Enforcement Administration chief Thomas Constantine. Constantine proposed to Congress that his agents could arrest doctors who use Oregon's death-with-dignity law to help terminally ill patients die, but U.S. Attorney-General Janet Reno ruled against this proposal.

June 6. "Crown wants Morrison case to proceed: Ruling in patient's death 'bad in law.'" (Kevin Cox)

Report on Nova Scotia's prosecution service's decision to reinstate a murder change against Dr. Nancy Morrison, despite public sentiment in favor of Morrison.

May 15. "AIDS doctor released on bail: Généreux awaits appeal; misrepresented self as caring, Crown says." (Donn Downey)

Maurice Généreux, who has been sentenced to two years less a day after he pleaded guilty to assisting a suicide, has been released on bail and is awaiting the result of an appeal of his sentence. Article describes details of his case.

May 14. "Doctor jailed 2 years for helping man kill himself: Patients depressed after HIV test given lethal dose of pills; Généreux sentence upsets Crown, defense." (Henry Hess)

Dr. Maurice Généreux has been sent to jail and is now the first physician in North America to be convicted of assisted suicide. Article reports the details of the case and the court proceedings, including the arguments put forth by the defense and the prosecution, and the testimony of Généreux's psychiatrist.

May 2. "In Syosset, N.Y.: The tragedy of police-assisted suicide." (Todd Lewan)

Article reports that according to two recent studies, at least 10 percent of police shootings are assisted suicides by cops. Also describes many actual incidences in which people manipulate cops into shooting them.

April 23. "Doctor-assisted suicide not rare in U.S., study finds." (Anon.)

Article reports the findings of a study published in the *New England Journal of Medicine*, according to which one in 16 U.S. doctors have helped at least one patient commit suicide, and many more doctors would be willing to engage in physician-assisted suicide if it were legalized.

March 21. "Helping death: No one should go so ungently into that good night." (Derek Cassels)

Author defends the actions of Dr. Nancy Morrison by outlining the options available to her when she was confronted with the suffering of Paul Mills, and by suggesting that her course of action, prescribing a lethal dose of drugs, was the most humane. Also criticizes the medical community for not taking a lead in addressing the issue of doctor-assisted suicide.

March 13. "MD loses license after assisting suicide: Généreux barred for prescribing sleeping pills to patients who wanted to take their own lives." (Henry Hess)

Article reports that the College of Physicians and Surgeons of Ontario has revoked Maurice Généreux's license to practice medicine after he admitted prescribing sleeping pills to patients who wanted to kill themselves. Article describes the proceedings of the hearing, as well as his "checkered" career.

March 7. "A time to die: Medical cases such as that involving Dr. Nancy Morrison stir strong feelings in people who wish a dying friend or relative and been kept alive longer—or let go sooner. How do we determine the line between relieving pain and hastening death?" (John Saunders)

Provides personal testimonies of individuals who, while not ethically opposed to "mercy killing" or "assisted suicide," are concerned that medical personnel are playing God and too much influenced by economic constraints in their decisions regarding end-of-life issues for their patients. There is focus on the need to talk frankly with patients and their families about end-of-life decisions. There is also talk about the principle of double effect, and the difference between administering drugs to alleviate suffering, or to hasten death, focusing on the issue of intent. Article attempts to be objective, but seems reluctant to endorse assisted suicide as a practice because of the inherent potential for abuses.

February 28. "Murder charge against Halifax doctor dismissed: Discharge reopens issue of treating dying patients." (Kevin Cox)

Report on Nova Scotia Provincial Court's decision to dismiss charges against Dr. Nancy Morrison due to lack of evidence.

February 27. "Husband defends helping elderly wife end life: First Manitoban charged with aiding suicide says spouse wanted unrelenting pain to stop." (David Roberts)

Article reports the details of an interview with Bert Doerksen, 79, the first Manitoban charged with aiding suicide. His wife, Susan, sought an escape from chronic pain.

February 21. "AIDS doctor who aided suicide had history of trouble: Watchdog lifted MD's license suspension." (Henry Hess)

Article describes the life, medical career and misconduct of Dr. Maurice Généreux, the first Canadian doctor to be convicted of assisting suicide. Although Généreux continues to practice, it is expected that he will be stripped of his license after the College of Physicians and Surgeons of Ontario meet for a disciplinary hearing.

February 9. "MD's murder hearing to put euthanasia on trial." (Kevin Cox)

Article marks the beginning of proceedings in the case against Dr. Nancy Morrison, who has been charged with killing a terminally ill cancer patient, Paul Mills. Debate about euthanasia has arisen as a result, and the practices and procedures of Victoria General Hospital are expected to be put on trial. Article notes that it is not publicly known exactly how Mills died.

February 3. "'Who are we to decide?' M.P. asks of euthanasia: Debate on private member's motion gets personal for some." (Anne McIlroy)

MP expresses concern regarding "euthanasia and doctor-assisted suicide," given his own experience with his severely handicapped son. He is concerned about how such laws might impact those who cannot speak for themselves. Detractors argue that safeguards could and should be put into place to handle such cases.

February 3. "Quebec fighting high suicide rate: Government sets aside additional $700,000 for prevention programs, public education." (Anon.)

Article looks for explanations for Quebec's disturbingly high suicide rate, including socioeconomic conditions and ongoing constitutional debate. Education is suggested as a means to counter this problem.

1997

December 23. "Nurse present at scores of assisted deaths: Making aided suicide legal would ensure 'proper consultation,' activist says." (John Saunders)

Toronto nurse suffering from terminal illness confesses to being present at scores of assisted deaths, and reveals plans to terminate her own life, stating individuals have the right to choose "euthanasia or assisted suicide," and the medical community should make provisions to safely assist individuals in their endeavors. Article also briefly cites objections from the Canadian Association for Suicide Prevention.

December 23. "MD admits assisting suicide: Doctor to be sentenced in March on two counts of aiding patients who wanted to die." (Henry Hess)

Toronto AIDS doctor is convicted of helping a patient commit suicide. Focuses more on alleged questionable character of defendant, than ethical issues surrounding "assisted suicide."

December 3. "Latimer's sentence on trial (II)." (Anon.)

Opinion piece says Latimer did not deserve a diluted sentence for "killing" his daughter Tracy, questioning Latimer's motives and issues of consent. Says debates surrounding "compassion-motivated murders" belong in Parliament and not before the courts.

December 2. "Latimer's sentence on trial (I)." (Anon.)

Opinion piece claims that public support for Latimer says important things about our culture, its arguing the necessity of having a *Charter* to protect the rights of persons who are disabled and those unable to speak for themselves.

December 2. "Why Latimer was sentenced to only two years." (Anon.; includes "The Jury's questions," excerpt from judge's ruling)

Excerpt from the decision of Mr. Justice Ted Noble, of the Court of Queen's Bench Saskatchewan, who reduced the sentence of Robert Latimer on constitutional grounds citing the unique circumstances of the case and characterizing Latimer's sentence as unconstitutional "cruel and unusual punishment." Also published with "The Jury's Questions," which describes how Noble notes the jury's concern for Latimer, and their inclination toward lenient sentencing.

December 2. "Exemptions rarely needed, experts say: Mandatory sentences disappearing as judges given penalty latitude for most crimes." (Kirk Makin)

Legal observers react to the constitutional exemption following from the Latimer decision, arguing the decision has set a frightening precedent. Generally sympathetic to Latimer verdict.

December 2. "Latimer receives 1 year in jail: Judge waives life sentence." (David Roberts)

Report of judge's decision to grant a constitutional exemption of Canada's mandatory life sentence for murder in the case of Robert Latimer. Reflects a relatively balanced treatment of the case with reactions on both sides of the issue, although a slight majority of quotes appear to be from detractors of the sentence. Article does not directly refer to assisted suicide.

November 8. "Parliament and assisted suicide." (Anon.)

Reports on Oregon voters' decision to legalize "assisted suicide" and seeming Canadian favor for protecting individual right to choice.

October 18. "A kinder, gentler way to suicide." (Arnott Weber)

Opinion piece is a satirical discussion of how we should extend the same basic courtesies to the terminally ill as to criminals if the "terminally disenchanted" individuals choose to end their lives through "physician assisted suicide," thus likening assisted suicide to capital punishment, both being viewed as stated-sanctioned murder.

August 14. "Japanese parents wonder who will look after them: As the baby-boom generation approaches retirement, untraditional children are no longer sharing their homes and caring for older family members." (Nicholas Kristof)

Article notes how Japanese attitudes toward the elderly and filial piety are changing, and how this is affecting families and the expectations of the elderly as to who will care for them as they age.

July 20. "Is Robert Latimer's life sentence 'cruel and unusual punishment'?" (Anon.)

Excepts from the decision of the Saskatchewan Court of Appeal in the Robert Latimer case, upholding the decision wherein Latimer was convicted of murdering his 12-year-old daughter, who suffered from cerebral palsy. Majority defers to parliamentary wisdom, and focuses on intentional nature of the act, while dissent claims sentence is cruel and unusual. Majority characterizes daughter's handicap as motivation for Latimer's action while dissent characterizes his motivation as the alleviation of suffering. Article refers to Latimer's act as homicide, but also points to a need for a third Criminal Code category for mercy killings.

May 31. "N.S. hospital administrator takes leave." (Anon.)

Administrator at hospital where Dr. Nancy Morrison works takes indefinite leave in order to join the external review process.

May 10. "Health & the aged." (Anon.)

Short reports on various issues affecting health and the aged, including the burden being taken off health care costs given that more elderly are choosing to die at home, a report that elderly with cancer are likely to take their own lives, and that elderly drivers killed in auto accidents tend to show signs of early Alzheimer's according to Swedish and Finnish studies.

May 9. "M.D.'s death role: Murder or mercy?" (Timothy Appleby and Jill Mahoney)

Discussion of the Nancy Morrison case and the continuing debate surrounding "euthanasia and assisted suicide" (described as two very different terms). Indicates that there are widely different public opinions and concerns surrounding the issue. Provides something of a Canadian legal history of assisted suicide, citing recent legal cases that have brought the issue to the fore.

May 9. "Families wondering if relatives killed." (Kevin Cox)

Morrison case prompts a wave of inquiries from survivors surrounding the deaths of their own loved ones, leading to rash of reviews and inquiries. Public begins to question medical wisdom, authority and practice.

May 8. "Doctor charged with murder." (Kevin Cox)

Report on Nancy Morrison, the first doctor in Canada to face a first-degree murder charge in connection with a patient death. Basic report on the events leading up to the charges, and the basic legal issues called into question.

April 19. "H.M.O.s: Health service or horror show? (Jane Coutts)

Review of *Health Against Wealth*, book outlining shortcomings in American health care system. Book is critical of H.M.O.s, and is reported as being full of horrifying anecdotal stories detailing the ills of the present system.

April 19. "When Mr. D calls, get ready to dance." (Moira Farr)

Review of *Denial of the Soul*, which opposes assisted suicide and legalized euthanasia as being against "God's higher purpose for each human individual" and *Dancing with Mr. D*, written by an Amsterdam nursing home doctor; two new books on death and end-of-life issues.

February 4. "Doctor faces new charges: Hearing delayed in case of AIDS patient's suicide and physician's actions." (Henry Hess)

Canadian doctor charged with helping a patient commit suicide will also be charged in connection with another attempted suicide. Reports on the details leading up to the case.

1996

September 26. "Man dies under euthanasia law." (Anon.)

Report on the death of a terminally ill man, the first to die under Australia's Northern Territory's law permitting "voluntary euthanasia."

August 24. "Front-line resistors fight Kevorkian's easy death." (Nat Hentoff)

Details the response of disabled activists to recent U.S. Ninth and Second Circuit Court decisions potentially legalizing assisted suicide, and acquitting Kevorkian. Disabled activists voice concerns that debates about quality-of-life issues will fail to respect that people with disabilities, with what may be regarded as diminished quality of life, still may lead complete and fulfilling lives.

August 10. "Verdicts on verdicts about easeful death." (Martin Levin)

In light of recent legal activity surrounding assisted suicide, author reviews several recent articles addressing the problem of assisted suicide, outlining the arguments of various writers.

June 21. "Doctor charged in man's suicide." (Jane Coutts and Henry Hess)

Report on Toronto AIDS specialist charged with assisting in the death of one of his patients, believed to be the first case of a Canadian doctor charged with this offence. Describes the details of the situation leading up to the charge, and of the checkered ethical history of the accused.

May 9. "Bastable tried to 'wake up Parliament.'" (Donn Downey)

Article on Austin Bastable, Canadian suffering from a degenerative disease who sought the help of American doctor Jack Kevorkian to help him end his life, allegedly as a last resort, having had little success in attempting to prompt the Canadian government to address the issue of "assisted suicide." Also presents the opinions of detractors of assisted suicide. Points to the need for government attention to this issue.

May 9. "Doctor Death ignores legalities on mission of mercy." (Timothy Appleby)

Portrait of Kevorkian as maverick crusader, actively looking for patients to facilitate his project. Points to Kevorkian's key role in raising publicity surrounding this issue. Presents a picture of Kevorkian as being somewhat unstable, and perhaps not the most credible spokesperson for "assisted suicide."

April 3. "M.D.s can aid suicides, U.S. Court rules." (Anon.)

Report on New York decision with short discussion of previous Washington decision and the Kevorkian trials of Michigan. Also reports opinion of Canadian Supreme Court Justice that this is an issue for lawmakers and not for the courts to decide.

1995

July 29. "Australian euthanasia legislation sparks mixture of relief, rage." (Philip Shenon)

Balanced discussion of pros and cons of Australia's Northern Territories' newly enacted legalization of "euthanasia."

June 10. "Depression as a healthy response." (Stanley Jacobson)

Practicing psychiatrist editorializes on how coming to terms with one's mortality is essential to the mental health of an aging person and population, despite the cultural taboos of discussing the same. He argues that not coming to terms with mortality is a key cause of depression in the elderly. Article does not speak directly to assisted suicide.

June 8. "Senate report on euthanasia: pro and con: On the big issue, the committee turned chicken." (Arthur Schafer)

Editorials expressing pro and con positions surrounding the Canadian Senate Committee on Euthanasia Report, also features "The Terms of the Debate," which outlines Report's working definitions of assisted suicide and euthanasia, discussing differences in the definitions and the moral implications allegedly inherent in these distinctions. Author points to the difficulty of making fine distinctions regarding moral problems, but suggests that the same is possible and necessary. Argues that the Committee suffered from a failure of nerve. Claims that public support for euthanasia and assisted suicide demands addressing problems surrounding the debate and finding ways to resolve the same. He suggests trial legalization.

June 8. "Senate report on euthanasia: pro and con: The committee was right to come out against legalizing euthanasia." (Ian Gentles)

Editorials expressing pro and con positions surrounding the Canadian Senate Committee on Euthanasia Report, also features "The Terms of the Debate," which outlines the Report's working definitions of assisted suicide and euthanasia, discussing differences in the definitions and the moral implications allegedly inherent in these distinctions. Gentles argues that despite seeming public favor, there is great protestation against euthanasia and assisted suicide from diverse members of the medical and religious communities. He argues that there are good reasons why the law in this area has remained untouched, and should remain unaltered. Although author uses each of the words, "euthanasia" and "assisted suicide," he seems to conflate them conceptually.

May 4. "How will the Senate Committee see assisted suicide?" (John Hofsess)

Commentary on anticipated Senate's Special Committee on Euthanasia and Assisted Suicide Report, arguing for personal choice despite Committee testimonies opposing legalization. Characterizes debate as question of who should control and regulate death: individual persons or a palliative care industry of experts. Rejects an art or science of palliative care that would allow an industry to gain control over such personal matters.

1994

March 8. "Challenging the Oath of Hippocrates." (Burnley McDougall)

Opinion piece questions the role of doctors and the Hippocratic Oath in light of "euthanasia" issue. Disdainfully characterizes new medicine as a return to a paganism, sanctioning the physician's right to kill as well as to cure.

1993

May 20. "Rodriguez' final question: Who owns my life?" (Deborah Wilson)

Report on considerations in the case of Sue Rodriguez, a Canadian woman with ALS seeking a constitutional exemption from Canadian Criminal Code prohibitions against "assisted suicide." Speaks from Rodriguez' point of view, telling of the progression of her illness and of her cogent decision to partake in assisted suicide. Battle characterized as centering around question of who owns one's life. Religious-based opposition is presented in a not-too-convincing manner.

February 10. "Dutch soften law on euthanasia." (Anon.)

Report on Dutch movement for legalization of euthanasia after years of having the practice in widely accepted legal limbo. Details euthanasia guidelines adopted by the Dutch, and provides pros and cons surrounding the issue, overall maintaining a balanced to favorable report for supporters of the issue.

1992

November 5. "U.S. doctors urge new policy allowing assisted suicides." (Anon.)

Report on *New England Journal of Medicine*'s urging for new public policy allowing physician-assisted suicide. Lists six recommendations to be included in such policy making, thus introducing many of the continuing considerations in assisted-suicide debate.

April 8. "Waiting for that final visitor." (Donn Downey)

Personal account of author's mother-in-law's deteriorating health and family's struggle to help her die with dignity. Details her painful and humiliating decline in health and living standards, describing her life as reduced to "waiting for death."

February 27. "Killing off the right to die." (John Hofsess)

Strong opinion piece reports defeat of bill C-203, designed to amend the Canadian Criminal Code to permit terminally ill patients to refuse medical treatment, and protecting doctors who would carry out such directives. Blames public apathy for contributing to unfortunate defeat. Identifies issue as something that cannot be much longer ignored.

February 6. "Doctor charged with murder in assisted suicides." (Anon.)

Disinterested report on Kevorkian's charges on two counts of murder is without urgency, emotional confusion or complication that will belie later articles on Kevorkian. Outlines legal question of differentiating assisted suicide and homicide without editorial commentary.

January 7. "When merely staying alive is morally intolerable." (Jim Lavery)

Report on Quebec Superior Court's decision to grant request of terminally ill patient Nancy B. to turn off the mechanical ventilator keeping her alive. Having withdrawn consent, Ms. B. was to this point being treated against her will. Case is significant because it creates a legal precedent in Canada relating to "euthanasia." Closes as opinion piece on difficulty of determining medically appropriate treatments, arguing for rights of individuals to make such decisions.

1991

November 29. "Destroying one life to end another." (Helen Lightbown)

Response to November 19 article "If mercy killing becomes legal" by Ian Gentles. Woman discusses legal and other risks she discovered in researching suicide options with her terminally ill mother. Discusses the frustrating impediments for individuals seeking to end their lives with dignity. Argues in favor of individual rights to determine end of life issues, including "euthanasia."

November 19. "If mercy killing becomes legal." (Ian Gentles)

Author opines that we should be suspect of "euthanasia" including "voluntary active euthanasia" based on slippery slope arguments, and a consideration of Dutch abuses, expressing concern with corruption if "mercy killing" becomes legal.

November 13. "Euthanasia backed in report." (Rod Mickelburgh)

Report on British Columbia Royal Commission on Health Care's favorable treatment of "euthanasia" and the right to die with dignity, along with outlining various other recommendations by the Commission.

October 21. "Voters get say on right to die." (Murray Campbell)

Discussion of upcoming Washington vote on the legalization of "doctor-assisted suicide" or "euthanasia," indicating seeming public support of the issue and detailing recent developments surrounding the issue. Although attempts to provide balanced report, seems to favor assisted suicide as a right.

September 14. "The right to die: Going gently." (Oakland Ross)

Anecdotal account of couple involved in joint suicide, leading to discussions on what constitutes a good death, and how issues of "euthanasia" and "suicide" are increasing subjects of public debate. Characterizes active and passive euthanasia, reviews Dutch experiences with decriminalization, upcoming Washington vote and palliative care in covering recent developments surrounding the issue. Argues Canadian opinion on "assisted suicide" remains divided.

September 14. "A farewell in Amsterdam." (Tony Sousa)

Personal story of death of author's Dutch friend who had him-self "euthanized" as sanctioned under Dutch law. Describes death as planned and dignified.

August 14. "Suicide: A part of everyday life?" (Alanna Mitch-ell)

Report of overall increase in suicide rate, and changing ideolog-ical and social factors that may be contributing to said increase.

June 24. "Against the dying of the light." (Joan Skelton)

Opinion piece details a woman's coming to terms with her moth-er's aging, and their attempts to find adequate care options for the elderly woman. Powerful descriptive account of the indigni-ties that can be inflicted on the elderly.

March 27. "Suicide rate for men jumps 42 percent in 20 years." (Anon.)

Report on study detailing increase in suicide and providing some explanations for the same, including lack of emotional support for and among men.

1990

December 15. "The legal response to assisting a suicide." (Anon.)

Report on American Court responses to end-of-life issues, in-cluding Kevorkian and Cruzan cases, drawing distinctions be-tween "active and passive euthanasia" and examining present Canadian legal stance on the issue of "assisting one commit sui-cide" or "mercy killing." Demands that parliament address this legal question.

August 16. "Treading the finest of lines." (Arthur Schafer)

Opinion piece motivated by CBC radio show on "euthanasia"/ "mercy killing" draws comparisons with British treatment of is-sue. Describes theological bent to Canadian discussion and fo-cus on slippery slope arguments in Britain. Opines that drugs hastening death should be available to terminally ill patients whose right to self-determination must be protected.

August. "What price immortality?" (Michael Bliss; *Report on Business Magazine*)

Argues that Canadians must learn to cost control their universal health care system, citing the United States for examples of cost containment measures. Author argues that economically speaking, Americans are being more realistic than idealistic Canadians at creatively addressing the economic realities of advancing medical technologies. He claims Canadian values and expectations must change in keeping with altering technological and economic realities, hence the need to set limits on our desire to live and our economic capacities to facilitate this desire. The author argues in favor the American model, despite its acknowledged unpopularity among Canadians.

June 30. "For mercy's sake." (Patrick Martin)

Discusses increasing societal interest in end-of-life issues, and Parliament's evasion of the same. Characterizes "passive and active euthanasia," providing balanced, thoughtful, comprehensive discussion of arguments from proponents and detractors. Argues Canadian Criminal Code should be amended to allow for regulated "physician aid in dying."

June 6. "MD admits assisting at suicide." (Anon.)

Report of death of Alzheimer's patient facilitated by Kevorkian's "suicide device," and impending the legal decision on whether he will be criminally charged in the death.

June 5. "Is a long life always the best life?" (Thomas Hurka)

Discusses quality-of-life issues in light of advances in medical technologies that prolong life. Questions what we value about life, and how long we should struggle to maintain physical existence.

1989

July 24. "When the choice is to die." (Anon.)

Opinion piece following study indicating suicide rate among elderly is rising. Seeks to repudiate medical wisdom that life is better when it is longer.

The New York Times Articles

1999

November 16. "Ex-nurse sentenced to 360 years in killings." (Bill Dedman)

The prosecution and sentencing of ex-nurse Orville Majors is reported, along with the details of the case. The author attempts to present Mr. Majors' side, but makes it fairly obvious that there is more implying his guilt than his innocence, and stresses the "evil" behind the crimes.

October 30. "Meddling with Oregon's law." (Anon.)

Article reports the passing of a bill by the House of Representatives making it a crime for doctors to prescribe lethal drugs to aid terminally ill patients to end their lives. The author highlights the distinction between a drug dose to alleviate pain at "the risk of death" and "for the purpose of causing death."

October 29. "Leave the personal to the States." (Charles Fried)

Author argues that the passing of a bill banning use of medicine in assisted suicide is not the business of the Congress, but rather the state. Main argument is that Congress' power in such an area is limited in the same way that it is unable to pass a low banning the death penalty.

October 29. "Oregon chafes at measures to stop assisted suicide." (Sam Howe Verhovek)

Article discusses the reaction of Oregon residents to Senate bill banning use of medicine in assisting suicide. Oregon is the only state to legalize physician-assisted suicide. The overwhelming reaction is affirmation of states' rights and anger at the implication that Oregon does not have the right to decide the assisted suicide issue for itself.

October 28. "House backs ban on using medicine to aid in suicide." (Robert Pear)

Article reports on the results of the vote to ban use of medicine in assisted suicide, noting that 71 Democrats joined 200 Republicans in passing the bill. It is noted that the penalty for prescribing drugs for the purpose of death is 20 years in prison and debates effect of such a decision on state policy making.

October 28. "Oregon considers challenge." (Sam Howe Verhovek)

A discussion of the possibility of elected officials in Oregon mounting a constitutional challenge to banning use of medicine in assisted suicide.

October 27. "Pope describes his feelings in unusual letter to the aged." (Alessandra Stanley)

Article reports and quotes extensively the recent letter released by Pope John Paul II on the subject of aging and the lives of the elderly. The Pope condemns euthanasia.

October 25. "Many doctors support lying to help patients." (Anon.)

Results of a survey reporting that a substantial number of doctors consider it ethical to lie to patients needing life-support procedures.

October 18. "Nurse guilty of killing six of his patients." (Bill Dedman)

Article reports the conviction of former nurse Orville Majors on six counts of first-degree murder for giving elderly patients lethal injections. It is implied that Majors' motivation for giving the injections is his alleged belief that the elderly are "a waste."

September 23. "Study finds shortcomings in care for chronically ill." (Sheryl Gay Stolberg)

Article reports research results showing that disproportionate medical attention paid to cancer patients has left those caring for the (otherwise) chronically ill with a heavy burden. It is theorized that because the chronically ill are reliant on others for long periods of time, they have a larger number of unmet needs and often must rely on paid assistance.

September 22. "Protest over Princeton's new ethics professor." (Neil MacFarguhar)

Article discusses the protest raised in reaction to Princeton's appointment of Mr. Peter Singer as the university's first bioethics professor. Opposition to Mr. Singer is due to his belief that euthanasia in the case of some disabled infants is appropriate when death involves less suffering than life.

September 5. "Kevorkian associate sought on murder charge." (Reuters)

Article reports the recently issued arrest warrant for Dr. Georges Reding, an associate of Dr. Kevorkian, for failing to appear in court on a first-degree murder charge rooted in the assisted suicide case of Ms. Donna Brennan. The author recalls previous charges against both Dr. Reding and Dr. Kevorkian that were dropped due to insufficient evidence.

September 5. "Gaps seen in the treatment of depression in the elderly." (Sara Rimer)

Article briefly describes the progress of an (unnamed) 92-year-old woman who was suicidal until she started using an anti-depressant. Author presents the possible situation of a neglectful national health care with relation to the elderly. Article does depict the side of those who believe that many doctors prescribe medication too hastily, but is more sympathetic toward the view of psychiatrists who believe that too many elderly go undiagnosed. Author touches on higher costs of treating depression, both for the individual, as well as the national health care system.

September 4. "Terminal cancer patients' will to live is found to fluctuate." (Erica Goode)

Article reports on a new study by Canadian researchers that suggests that a terminal cancer patient's will to live fluctuates substantially, and is related to specific factors that shift over time. The study is shown to be significant due to its being the first source of "quantified," "empirical" data about dying patients.

August 31. "Trial opens for ex-nurse charged in Indiana killings." (Bill Dedman)

Article reports the opening of the trial of an ex-nurse accused of killing seven elderly patients at the Clinton hospital in Indiana. Details are given about the connection between an abnormally high death rate in the intensive care unit and when the ex-nurse was on duty. A possible motive is described to be disdain toward the elderly.

August 17. "A view of 'the other side' through dying patients' eyes." (Timothy E. Quill, M.D.)

A doctor's personal account of two past patients who recalled near-death experiences. The author reveals his fascination by such recollections, and reflects that they reinforce his passion for his job as a healer.

August 11. "The Netherlands: Legalizing euthanasia." (Anon.)

Article reports new legislation in the Netherlands that will legalize euthanasia to anyone over the age of 12, changing a practice that has previously been confined to adults.

August 10. "First, do no harm: When patients suffer." (Sandeep Jauhar, M.D.)

A doctor reports evidence showing that due to "adverse events" during hospital stays, some patients may have higher chances of recovery with minimum medical intervention. Statistics are given showing the percentage of patients who experience adverse events, and those most common.

August 7. "Man accused of assisting wife's suicide." (Susan Sachs)

Article reports the arraignment of Mr. Peter Florio, charged with second-degree manslaughter for helping his ill wife commit suicide by attaching a rope to a ceiling beam in their apartment. The article touches on the low rate of convictions of assisted suicide cases in New York, as well as the issue of what exactly counts as assistance.

July 29. "Surgeon General opens campaign to counter rise in suicide." (Anon.)

Article reports the declaration by the U.S. Surgeon General of suicide as a serious public health threat, marking the event as the first mental health issue ever to be addressed. Educating the public is reported to be the most significant preventative strategy in the Surgeon General's report.

July 29. "Husband pleads guilty in 'mercy killing' of wife." (Anon.)

Brief article reports 87-year-old Mr. Walter Papeman of Rockland County pleading guilty to the charge of second-degree manslaughter in the shooting of his wife. The death has been viewed as a mercy killing and will land him no more than one year in jail.

July 27. "The aged as an inconvenience." (Ann R. Langdon)

Editorial discusses society's attitude toward the elderly as being neglectful, and shows doctors and staff at nursing homes to be only in search of ways to lessen their own hassles. The author questions the hasty turn to pharmacological solutions in many cases, and warns that those who have this attitude will receive the same treatment in the future.

July 21. "Organ transplant panel urges a broad sharing of livers." (Sheryl Gay Stolberg)

A detailed look at the effort to resolve the dispute over who should get rare donated organs, spurred by a government-ordered regulation to revamp the allocation system privately run by the United Network for Organ Sharing. The article is interspersed with references to a new system of allocation favoring the most medically urgent situations, while debating the old system's fairness.

July 17. "Grand jury refuses to indict in an assisted suicide." (Barbara Stewart)

Article reports the Manhattan jury verdict to not prosecute veterinarian Dr. Marco Zancope for injecting Cara Beigel, a dying friend, with a fatal drug dose. The author highlights the possibility of a more sympathetic jury in cases where the dying person is closer to death, and where the family of the dying is in support of the decision.

July 5. "Man killed his father in hospital out of mercy, official says." (Michael Cooper)

Article briefly reports the claim of Joseph Raineri, Jr. that his brutal attack on his father was a mercy killing, but concentrates mostly on the attack of his father's roommate, Michael D'Ambrose. The article is apologetic in nature in response to erroneous reports in earlier editions of *The Times* that Mr. D'Ambrose had died due to the attack.

May 26. "Woman avoids murder charge over daughter." (Rick Bragg)

Article reports the change of decision of prosecutors in Orange County to charge Georgette Smith's mother, Shirley Egan, with her death. Smith was paralyzed from the neck down after being shot by her mother, and chose to end her own life proceeding a successful lawsuit.

May 23. "Kevorkian appeal cites ineffective counsel." (Anon.)

A concise report of an attempt made by lawyer Mayer Morganroth to suggest that Dr. Kevorkian's murder conviction be thrown out due to bad legal advice. It is emphasized that though he was given advice throughout his trial, Dr. Kevorkian chose to represent himself.

May 19. "A family shooting and a twist like no other." (Rick Bragg)

A description of the debates that have arisen since the allowance of Georgette Smith to end her own life after being shot by her mother resulting in paralysis from the neck down. Article touches on the unusual circumstances of the case, where Smith conceded to help build a case against her mother in order to be allowed to die. Legal academics are consulted to consider whether Smith had an acceptable reason for refusing treatment, or whether her mother was not at all responsible for her death since she did not directly cause it.

May 11. "Reflecting on a life of treating the dying." (Sheryl Gay Stolberg)

An interview with Dame Cicely Saunders, the founder of Hospice, which specializes in end-of-life care. Saunders speaks of the beginnings of her training in the medical profession, and how she came to become compassionate toward the dying. Most significant to the American audience is her wariness about assisted suicide that she claims stems from her positive experience with what the dying can do with the end of their lives if they are in good care.

April 14. "Kevorkian sentenced to 10 to 25 years in prison." (Dirk Johnson)

Article reports on Judge Jessica Cooper's sentencing of Dr. Jack Kevorkian to 10 to 25 years in prison, and includes the judge's statement to Kevorkian in full. Article also documents the various reactions of those present to the sentence.

April 10. "Princeton's new philosopher draws a stir." (Sylvia Nasar)

Article reports on the negative reaction aroused by Peter Singer's appointment to a chair in bioethics at Princeton University's Center for Human Values, which is based at least partly on his belief that euthanasia for severely disabled infants can be justified in some cases.

April 9. "Books of the times: Distracting detours in the hunt for a final exit." (Michiko Kakutani)

Author reviews David Guterson's new novel, *East of the Mountains*, in which the main character is a retired doctor who suffers from colon cancer, because of which he plans to commit suicide.

March 30. "Kevorkian seen as 'distraction' on suicide aid." (Pam Belluck)

Article documents the speculations of various advocates and opponents to assisted suicide and euthanasia on the possible effect Kevorkian's conviction of second-degree murder will have on the assisted suicide and euthanasia debate.

March 27. "Dr. Kevorkian's luck runs out." (Anon.)

Author condemns Kevorkian for administering lethal injections to Thomas Youk himself, as opposed to allowing the patient to be in control of the lethal substance; author also regrets that many who seek assistance with suicide are forced to accept the services of such an "odd character" as Dr. Kevorkian.

March 27. "Dr. Kevorkian is a murderer, the jury finds: He faces 10 to 25 years in dying man's death." (Pam Belluck)

Article reports that Kevorkian's murder trial has resulted in him being convicted of second-degree murder. It also reports on Kevorkian's reaction to the verdict, the reactions of others present at the trial, the reactions of leaders of different activist groups, as well as the thoughts of one of the jurors.

March 26. "Kevorkian appeals to emotions of jurors as they begin weighing murder charges: Theatrical closing arguments to make up for shortcomings." (Pam Belluck)

Article reports on the closing arguments of both the prosecution and Dr. Kevorkian in his murder trial, as well as reviews the details of the case and the trial.

March 25. "Dr. Kevorkian's client." (Anon.)

Author ridicules Dr. Kevorkian's attempt to act as his own defense attorney, but admits that it is not yet clear whether the jury will convict him.

March 25. "Kevorkian rests case without calling witnesses." (Anon.)

Article reports that Kevorkian rested his case without calling any witnesses in his murder trial, since he was not permitted to appeal to the pain and suffering of the terminally ill man to whom he administered lethal injections.

March 24. "Kevorkian stumbles in his self-defense: Doctor's lack of legal skill becomes evident in his murder trial." (Pam Belluck)

Article documents the many problems faced by Kevorkian in attempting to defend himself in his murder trial.

March 23. "Kevorkian says his role in death was 'duty.'" (Andrew Bluth)

Article outlines the line of defense that Kevorkian will use in his murder trial, which is based on the notion that he has a certain duty as a physician. Article also details the events leading up to the trial, and examines the fact that Kevorkian is representing himself.

March 20. "For Kevorkian, a fifth, but very different, trial; Kevorkian and the state face higher stakes in a fifth trial; for the first time, the doctor is charged with first-degree murder." (Pam Belluck)

Article outlines the differences between Kevorkian's upcoming trial, where he is being charged with first-degree murder, and his previous four trials, where he was accused of violating laws prohibiting assisted suicide. Article also examines the significance of the videotape that shows Kevorkian injecting a fatal solution into Thomas Youk, as well as the question of whether Kevorkian will be representing himself at the trial.

March 8. "Tips from Jimmy Carter on living well in old age." (Sara Rimmer)

Article reports on Jimmy Carter's latest book, *The Virtues of Aging*, and the American Society on Aging's annual conference. As keynote speaker, one of the themes discussed by Carter was the end of life; he said that he and his wife had signed living wills stating that they do not want to be kept alive by artificial means.

February 27. "When doctors go too far; my relatives suffered; Medicare paid the bill." (Schulyer Bishop)

Author suggests a connection between doctors who are overzealous in their attempts to extend life and the prospect of hospitals and doctors claiming money from Medicare, by outlining four cases of family members who were kept alive despite pain and desires to the contrary, while Medicare paid for their treatment.

February 18. "Oregon reporting 15 deaths in 1998 under suicide law; officials see no abuses; but findings reignite debate over doctors' prescribing lethal doses of drugs." (Sam Howe Verhovek)

Article cites the results of the Health Division's official report on Oregon's Death With Dignity Act, which makes doctor-assisted suicide legal, and which completed its first full year in 1998. Advocates of the law claim that the results of the report are evidence of the law's success; however, traditional opponents of assisted suicide, such as Archbishop John Vlazny, have not been swayed by the results.

February 16. "Personal health: At life's end, patients want their wishes to be heard." (Jane E. Brody)

Article details a study, published in *The Journal of the American Medical Association*, which reports on what patients consider to be appropriate care for the end of life. The five main suggestions made by patients include: avoiding pointless prolongation of life, retaining control of decisions while possible, sparing loved ones serious burdens (including having to make decisions about treatment), being fully involved with loved ones in talking about dying and receiving adequate treatment for pain.

1998

December 10. "Judge orders Kevorkian to be tried for murder." (Anon.)

Dr. Kevorkian is the first to challenge a new Michigan law banning assisted suicide by aiding in the death of 52-year-old Thomas Youk. In hopes of bringing the assisted suicide debate to a higher level, Dr. Kevorkian even provides prosecutors with a videotape of him administering the man with the fatal injection.

November 29. "Kevorkian's hope is for jury sympathy, lawyers say." (Maggie Fox)

Fox argues that jury perception of Kevorkian's intent will be the determining factor in Kevorkian's first-degree murder trial, following the televised euthanization of terminally ill Thomas Youk. Argues that Kevorkian's actions are unquestionably illegal but that jury may be swayed by more emotional and intuitive considerations that will be couched in terms of legal intent. Article also provides a brief statistical and demographic synopsis of present opinions regarding assisted suicide. Note again unfavorable treatment of Kevorkian's character.

November 28. "Beliefs: Wide-ranging, tough questions have been provoked by the broadcast of Kevorkian's video." (Peter Steinfels)

Following televised Kevorkian assisted suicide, Steinfels questions the sensationalism of the television episode and its efficacy in forwarding the debate on assisted suicide. He calls into question broadcasters' attempts to cover both sides of the issue and argues that journalistic questioning of figures involved did little to forward the debate or to challenge viewers philosophically or ideologically. Steinfels attempts to reorient the debate back to its ethical and philosophical origins and warns of the issue deteriorating to a circus sideshow focused around media sensationalism.

November 27. "Kevorkian legal plan faulted." (Anon.)

Former Kevorkian lawyer challenges Kevorkian's judgment in choosing to represent himself at his upcoming first-degree murder trial in the death of Thomas Youk. Geoffrey Fieger questions Kevorkian's character, citing his temperamental nature and "self-destructive" impulses.

November 26. "Kevorkian faces a murder charge in death of man: Fallout from broadcast: Both sides praise decision by prosecutor to take debate on euthanasia to court." (Dirk Johnson)

Balanced report on first-degree murder charges brought against Kevorkian, following *60 Minutes* assisted suicide video, indicates that both sides of the debate are eager for the issue to enter the legal forum. Kevorkian's act itself is perceived as a defiant affront to the law, and calls his personal judgment into question. Kevorkian's choice to act as his own legal counsel is also challenged.

November 26. "Kevorkian case difficult to prosecute, experts say." (William Glaberson)

Discusses potential difficulties prosecutors may have in getting a guilty verdict in Kevorkian's murder charge following the televised euthanization of Thomas Youk, based on the consideration that jury sentiment is most likely to be the deciding factor in their decision. Challenges applicability of existing laws to treat of such ethically delicate and emotionally charged issues. Article indicates that this is problematic because whereas murder is usually indicative of a disregard for life, Kevorkian builds his case on the argument that his actions evidence a higher regard for human life. Raises the slippery slope issues that make the subject morally problematic.

November 25. "A televised death: Prurient or newsworthy, or both?" (Walter Goodman)

Article focuses on negative feedback following *60 Minutes* broadcast of Kevorkian-assisted suicide, but argues that regardless of one's opinion regarding the issue, CBS's success in drawing attention to the issue made it a journalistic success. Goodman argues, contra Steinfels, that journalists acted responsibly in drawing positive attention to a disturbing and morally problematic subject and that discomfort with the program is the result of its deep subject. Despite accolades for the broadcast, popularity of Kevorkian himself seems to be on the wane.

November 24. "Light sentence in mercy death is overturned in west Canada." (Anthony De Palma)

Canadian appellate court overturned a "light" sentence in the mercy killing case of Robert Latimer in favor of a tougher penalty. Fears of advocates for the disabled-rights groups are detailed alongside arguments of right-to-die proponents. Despite acknowledging the complexities of the issue, article claims that the Canadian Supreme Court will have to tackle this issue.

November 24. "Death 'appeared a homicide,' state says." (Bill Dedman)

Report discusses public reaction and potential legal responses following Kevorkian-assisted suicide televised on *60 Minutes* television program. Thomas Youk's assisted death is the first where Kevorkian does not use his "suicide machine" to facilitate death but directly administers lethal drugs to his patient. Prosecutors, acknowledging public sympathy for Kevorkian's cause, remain undecided whether he will be prosecuted despite Kevorkian's call for his own charge. Although Youk's family supports his decision and public interest in the issue is evidenced by high television ratings, Kevorkian's own character is called into question given his seemingly callous approach to the procedure and his desire to prompt legal response.

November 23. "Prosecutor to weigh possibility of charging Kevorkian." (Pam Belluck)

Report discusses factors to be considered as Michigan prosecutor deliberates whether to charge Kevorkian following his involvement in televised assisted death of Thomas Youk. Kevorkian is quoted as desiring to bring charges upon himself in order to engage in a legal "showdown." The article addresses factors, including consent, which will play a role in deciding whether to prosecute Kevorkian. Kevorkian's character is called into question given his suspiciously adamant desire to be prosecuted, his insensitivity during the procedure itself and his stated preference of administering drugs directly in the name of efficiency.

November 23. "*60 Minutes,* Kevorkian and a death for the cameras." (Caryn James)

Report on *60 Minutes* program that televised Kevorkian-assisted suicide questions Kevorkian's perceived insensitivity during the episode, which is depicted as a "stunt" on the part of Kevorkian. The article discusses larger issues of how personal issues such as death, sex and religion have recently "gone public" as also evidenced by the White House sex scandals, challenging the propriety of moving such private experiences as death into the public forum and the media's newfound fascination with intimate details of individual lives. The author argues that while videos of patient Youk's illness and physical degeneration are compelling, the "lurid sensationalism" of the production ultimately undermines the case for assisted suicide and detracts from the real issues at hand. Finally shifts question to whether, in light of such considerations, Youk in fact had a "good death."

November 20. "CBS to show Kevorkian video of man's death." (Felicity Barringer)

Brief report of CBS network plans to air Kevorkian-assisted suicide on upcoming *60 Minutes* television program. Reports on how similar subject matter was received when televised in 1994. Note somewhat unfavorable treatment of Kevorkian's character.

November 4. "Details doom assisted-suicide measures: Moving stories vs. legislative reality." (Yale Kamisar)

Although polls indicated that a majority of Michigan residents support assisted suicide, a proposal (Proposal B) supporting its legalization did not pass. Failure is attributed to both the blizzard of television and radio advertisements sponsored by opponents, and the difficulty of articulating the measure in acceptable form.

October 17. "Was it mercy or murder? Veterinarian's arrest puts focus on pacts to help the terminally ill commit suicide." (Jennifer Steinhauer)

An account of the case of Cara Beigel, a woman with terminal breast cancer whose life ended when a close friend, a veterinarian, injected her with lethal drugs at her request. Outlines the unusual aspects of this particular case, and describes the "gray areas" in which doctors operate when faced with requests for assisted suicide.

October 15. "Doctor is arraigned in assisted suicide: Veterinarian is said to admit role in terminally ill friend's death." (Randy Kennedy)

Reports the arraignment of Dr. Marco Zancope on a charge of second-degree manslaughter; Zancope has confessed to assisting in the suicide of Cara Beigel. This is only the second instance in New York City in which a person who assisted in a suicide has been prosecuted.

October 3. "Virginia's top court rejects appeal in right-to-die case." (Anon.)

Reports that the Virginia Supreme Court has rejected Governor James S. Gilmore's appeal to have Hugh Finn's feeding tube reinserted, on the grounds that removing the tube merely permits the natural dying process to take place, and is not an instance of mercy killing. Gives Gilmore's reasons for the appeal.

October 2. "Wife wins right-to-die case; then a Govenor challenges it." (Irvin Molotsky)

Reports that Governor James S. Gilmore III has ordered an appeal of the ruling that allows Michelle Finn to remove the feeding tube that has kept her husband, Hugh, alive in a vegetative state for over three years. The Associated Press reports that the feeding tube has been removed.

September 29. "Family will allow a comatose man to die." (Anon.)

The family of a man in a vegetative state have reversed their position and are now allowing his wife to remove the feeding tube that has sustained him for three and a half years. Comments were available from neither the State Human Resources Secretary nor the Attorney General.

September 17. "Overreaching on assisted suicide." (Anon.)

Editorial criticizing a new bill that would allow the Federal Drug Enforcement Administration to investigate and punish any physician who prescribes lethal doses of drugs with the intent of assisting in a patient's suicide. The bill is said to be an inappropriate attempt to undo the Oregon Death With Dignity Act.

August 19. "Legal suicide has killed 8, Oregon says: A report that offers a stark glimpse into legally assisted suicide." (Sam Howe Verhovek)

Provides statistics on the 10 people who have received state authorization to engage in doctor-assisted suicide since the Death With Dignity Act took effect (two of these people died before they received the lethal medication). A more extensive report will be made public early next year.

July 22. "Michigan to decide on doctor-aided suicide." (Anon.)

Reports that an advocacy group for doctor-assisted suicide has gathered enough signatures in Michigan to place a ballot initiative on the legality of the practice in the November elections.

July 19. "Patient's rights: Getting litigious with H.M.O.s: Three studies say the legal system fails injured patients." (Michael M. Weinstein)

Reports that the Democrats are backing a "patient bill of rights" that would enable all workers to sue their health maintenance organization for damages if they suffer injury because it refused to cover a treatment a doctor prescribed. Criticizes the present legal system for its inability to compensate injured patients and proposes three alternatives.

July 13. "One man's battle with the managed-care monster." (Thomas W. Self)

A gastroenterologist recounts his personal story of having been fired from his job for not succumbing to the pressures of the managed-care organization and the medical group to be less than thorough with his patients in order to cut costs.

July 6. "Largest H.M.O.'s cutting the poor and the elderly: A managed-care retreat: Insurers cite losses and low government payments in Medicaid and Medicare." (Peter T. Kilborn)

Report on how managed health care organizations are cutting programs for the poor and elderly due to economic losses and cuts, along with comments from health care providers. Provides an economically and somewhat politically focused discussion of the issue, without investigation into attendant ethical matters or patient responses.

July 4. "Ban on assisted suicide." (Anon.)

Brief report on Michigan legislature's approval of a bill banning assisted suicide, largely in response to the activities of Dr. Jack Kevorkian.

June 17. "Study finds pain of oldest is ignored in nursing homes." (Sheryl Gay Stolberg)

Reports on study indicating that elderly in nursing homes are being severely undertreated in terms of pain management, suggesting better palliative care strategies are required for managing aging and death. Points to demographic evidence that minorities are most negatively affected by this phenomenon, and speculates as to the causes of the overall trend.

June 8. "Assisted suicide, at state discretion." (Anon.)

Brief article applauding Justice Janet Reno's decision that physicians acting under Oregon's assisted suicide law could not be prosecuted by the D.E.A. Speaks openly against the right-to-life movement's attachment to this issue, and argues the importance of individual choice in this matter. Among the first reports with a decidedly biased flavor.

June 8. "Kevorkian offers organs in assisted-suicide case." (Anon.)

Brief report tells of Kevorkian's offering the kidneys of one of his patients for organ transplant. Outlines legal ramifications of Kevorkian's act and legal problems with donation of the organs. Appears a somewhat sensationalistic and potentially damaging action on the part of Kevorkian, at a juncture where assisted suicide seems to be coming more into public favor.

June 6. "Reno lifts barrier to Oregon's law on aided suicide: Overrules D.E.A. Chief: She won't prosecute doctors who prescribe doses to state's terminally ill." (Neil A. Lewis)

Report on U.S. Supreme Court ruling that doctors acting under Oregon's assisted-suicide law (the only one of its kind in the U.S.) were not to be prosecuted, thereby overruling a D.E.A. policy impeding the law. Provides reactions to the ruling, and draws parallels between assisted suicide and abortion.

May 7. "3-Doctor rule dropped in 'right to die' cases." (Anon.)

The New Jersey State Board of Medical Examiners agrees, after public hearings, to revise its requirement that three doctors determine the competency of a terminally ill patient refusing life sustaining treatment, in favor of a policy allowing the attending physician alone to determine competency.

May 2. "Beliefs: A longtime leader in biomedical ethics reflects on his field's explosive growth, the backlash against it and 'false hopes' in America's health care quest." (Peter Steinfels)

Author interviews Daniel Callahan, founder and retired director of the Hasting Center, a well-respected institute for the study of biomedical ethics. Interview focuses on the increased cultural concern for ethics, concerns of physicians and scientists that ethicists are impeding research progress and "false hopes" regarding the continuing ability to allocate equitable health care and resources. Callahan expresses the continuing need for ethicists' participation in debates. No direct reference to assisted suicide.

April 26. "In death, the goal is no questions asked." (Sheryl Gay Stolberg)

Discusses how the legal requirement to document death prompts a certain reluctance on the part of physicians to participate in "assisted suicide." She points out the continuing secrecy surrounding assisted suicide in light of these administrative and bureaucratic procedures.

April 24. "A change of heart on assisted suicide." (Diane E. Meier)

A medical practitioner writes about her revised opinion on assisted suicide, arguing that the risks do outweigh the benefits, and that even the most stringent regulation would be insufficient and subject to abuse. She suggests altering focus to reducing end-of-life suffering instead of hastening death.

April 23. "Assisted suicides are rare, survey of doctors finds: Patient requests denied: 5 percent admit giving injections—more say they would do so if procedure were legal." (Sheryl Gay Stolberg)

Investigates the frequency of "physician-assisted suicide," citing national survey finding that while patients often request the same, their requests are rarely carried out. Legal problems surrounding the issue are cited as the primary reason why doctors remain reluctant to honor patient requests to die. Stolberg points to the disparity between public support of physician-assisted suicide and medical reluctance to comply with patient wishes in the face of legal indeterminacies and corollary problems.

April 21. "Guide covers territory suicide law does not explore." (Sheryl Gay Stolberg)

Discussion of guidelines and terminology associated with Oregon's Death With Dignity Act permitting "physician-assisted suicide." Excerpts from guidelines for Death With Dignity Act are reprinted. Provides a window into the considerations of health care providers drafting guidelines and legislation, thus intimating their concerns surrounding the issue. There is an emphasis on providing full information and on the responsibilities of physicians in reporting and attending to the patient.

March 28. "A better death in Oregon." (Anon.)

The Oregon doctor-assisted suicide law is seen as an acknowledgment that "the idea of helping people expire has become less unthinkable than watching them die too slowly by being forced to live too long." Despite the acknowledged difficulties in forming such a law, the article suggests that voters have decided that officials need find ways to facilitate this kind of legislation.

March 28. "Hospital worker admits killing up to 50 patients, official says." (Anon.)

The California Respiratory Care Board suspends the license of a practitioner who confessed to "killing patients for humane reasons."

March 28. "Kevorkian delivers another body to hospital." (Anon.)

Kevorkian dropped off the body of a woman, suffering from Huntington's disease, to a Detroit hospital. The patient died shortly thereafter.

March 26. "First death under an assisted-suicide law: Moving a debate from the abstract to the actual." (Timothy Egan)

Report on the first death to take place under Oregon's Death With Dignity Act permitting "assisted suicide," followed by general discussion of assisted suicide and attendant issues.

March 11. "At the end of life, a blind bureaucracy." (Marilyn Webb)

Author discusses hospice care ideology that dying patients require emotional, spiritual, physical and mental support, disdaining lack of government support for such care given the changed, prolonged nature of dying in the modern world. Argues that the system needs to be revamped to cope with such realities.

March 7. "Beliefs: Doctor-assisted suicide in Oregon: An idea that complicates health care for the poor and challenges government neutrality." (Peter Steinfels)

Steinfels discusses the problematic notion of "assisted suicide" given the language of health care. He notes the bureaucratic problems in facilitating the law and the problems with making the law financially expedient, and to allow for its egalitarian application. Concludes that despite the very private nature of this kind of choice, it is also inevitably a matter for social and political debate and concern.

March 4. "As life ebbs, so does time to elect comforts of hospice." (Sheryl Gay Stolberg)

Author refers to the experience of one family to indicate how, given the confusion on issues surrounding death, patients are receiving inadequate, even "chaotic" care in their final days. Suggests that hospice care is a positive and viable means to facilitate a good death, but that the medical system needs to learn how and when to incorporate this kind of treatment into its program for caring for terminally ill patients.

February 10. "Elderly seek longer life, regardless." (Susan Gilbert)

Reports that elderly patients surveyed indicated that they desired to live despite diminishing life quality, and that this finding impacts understanding of the "death with dignity" debate. She points to the danger of assuming that one knows what a patient's desires may be, citing the survey's findings that patients' wishes are quite frequently misunderstood.

January 24. "Justice Dept. bars punishing Oregon doctors aiding suicides." (Anon.)

The U.S. Justice Department determines that federal drug officers are not able to punish doctors who help with suicides under Oregon's new "assisted suicide" law. The Drug Enforcement Administration is thus not to become involved with doctors acting under this law, removing an impediment that could trouble doctors, causing them to shy away from such treatment for fear of legal ramifications.

January 5. "When dying is as hard as birth." (Christina Walker Campi)

Author moves the focus of the "physician-assisted suicide" debate to questions of palliative care, recalling her own experiences in the death of several family members, and her confusion over related end-of-life decisions. She suggests we look to management of dying and death as much as treatment of illness.

1997

December 31. "Nurse with tender touch is held in six killings."
(Dirk Johnson)

Indiana nurse is held for "killing" six hospital patients. The patients tended to be elderly, but were listed as being in stable condition at the hospital.

December 22. "Medicare H.M.O.s to trim benefits for the elderly: Expenses are soaring: Cap on government payments is ending days of low fees and free prescriptions." (Milt Freudenheim)

Reviews some of the changes being made to Medicare H.M.O.s, focusing in particular on how these changes are adversely affecting the elderly, both financially through added premiums and otherwise. Article does not mention assisted suicide, but does question American handling of health coverage for an aging population.

November 13. "Clinton administration asks Supreme Court to rule against assisted suicide: Contrasting life support withheld and death brought about." (Linda Greenhouse)

The Clinton administration urges the Supreme Court to find that the American Constitution does not guarantee terminally ill individuals the right to a "physician-assisted suicide," drawing a distinction between allowing one to die and actively participating in hastening death.

October 26. "Assisted suicide comes full circle, to Oregon."
(Timothy Egan)

Report on Oregon's second vote regarding the legalization of "assisted suicide" (moving to repeal a law allowing the same) suggesting opponents of assisted suicide are running a well-financed campaign, based on slippery slope objections, although public sentiment in favor of the law is still high.

October 15. "Kevorkian lawyer cited in note on body." (Anon.)

Report on the discovery of a body in a Michigan hotel room, linked to Kevorkian.

October 15. "Assisted suicide clears a hurdle in highest court."
(Linda Greenhouse)

U.S. Supreme Court removes legal obstacles to the Oregon physician-assisted suicide law. Article discusses the Oregon law and the upcoming vote regarding its continuing legality.

September 24. "H.M.O.s seen as easing death for the elderly." (Anon.)

Discusses the effectiveness of H.M.O. plans in easing death for the elderly.

September 22. "Kevorkian in new suicide." (Anon.)

Reports of Kevorkian "attending the suicide" of a terminally ill Canadian man.

September 9. "Kevorkian is called irresponsible for role in woman's suicide." (Anon.)

Report of Kevorkian's involvement in the suicide of a woman alleged by her family to be mentally incompetent, thus unable to give proper consent.

September 2. "The face of the future in Japan: Economic threat of aging populace." (Sheryl WuDunn)

Article focuses on Japan as the world's most rapidly aging industrial society, and discusses the economic implications of caring for such an aging population.

August 2. "Rage against the dying of the light." (Ann Hood)

Author discusses her family's experiences with her terminally ill father, pointing to the myriad decisions they were faced with that could have been construed as contributing to assisting suicide. The article is not unsympathetic to assisted suicide, but is very effective in illustrating the complex and contingent nature of end-of-life decisions.

July 25. "Not dead enough to die: Laws force life support on a man who never could consent." (Esther B. Fein)

Anecdotal introduction discusses the issue of individuals who are not capable of providing consent regarding end-of-life decisions due to mental incompetence. The article seems sympathetic to the right of families to act as surrogates for individuals enduring undue suffering because of legal impediments that prolong their lives. Slippery slope arguments regarding "euthanasia" are cited by detractors.

July 24. "Assisted suicide? Not in my state." (Ezekiel Emanuel and Linda Emanuel)

Florida Supreme Court acknowledges that the Legislature could allow doctors to help patients die, given that a Supreme Court decision found no constitutional barrier to state legalization of "assisted suicide." Discusses deliberation of various states regarding "euthanasia." Suggests that while on the surface most Americans are in favor of assisted suicide, they become less fervent faced with some of the ethical dilemmas associated with the subject, revealing a covert reluctance to sanction the practice. The authors argue that, ultimately, we require better care for the terminally ill and not legalization of assisted suicide.

July 23. "When morphine fails to kill." (Gina Kolata)

Examines whether morphine actually hastens death in terminally ill patients, citing palliative care experts' allegations of evidence to the contrary. Experts argue against the common contention that morphine hastens death through causing respiratory problems, instead claiming patients develop a certain tolerance to extraordinarily high doses of the drug. Such evidence complicates arguments for assisted suicide based on the supposition that administering high doses of pain-regulating medication, such as morphine, is basically the same as facilitating death through administering lethal doses of drugs.

July 18. "Florida High Court upholds state ban on assisted suicide." (Anon.)

Florida upholds state law banning "physician-assisted suicide," although the Court leaves the door open for legislators to craft a law addressing this issue. Reported public reactions intimate favor for the legalization.

July 8. "Suicide brings to life a legal quandary: Ambiguities in case of a man charged with helping his wife to die." (Jonathan Rabinovitz)

Report on man charged with assisted suicide in the death of his wife. Generally sympathetic tone suggests that if husband was complicit in his wife's death, it was in keeping with her own wishes.

July 6. "Dying well is the best revenge." (Paul Wilkes)

Tells of individuals' attempt to control their own deaths. Focuses quality of life debates. Lengthy, although not entirely sympathetic, discussion of hospice care. Discusses one man's attempt to manage his own death, and the difficult decisions he faced in doing so.

July 6. "Appealing to the law's brooding spirit." (Linda Greenhouse)

Only passing reference to "assisted suicide" in article discussing the political aspects of how American Supreme Court judgments are crafted.

July 3. "Assisted suicide decision looms in Florida." (Mireya Navarro)

Reports of upcoming decision in Florida Supreme Court relating to assisted-suicide issue. Assisted-suicide issue is of special interest in Florida because of its aging population, and the growing concern over rising health care costs, although article indicates that the elderly have shown strong support for assisted suicide.

July 1. "Benchmarks of justice: In 9 extraordinary months, the High Court developed a vast panorama of landmarks." (Linda Greenhouse)

United States Supreme Court rules that there is no constitutional right to doctor-assisted suicide, thus leaving the issue for legislative development within the jurisdiction of the individual states.

June 30. "Wanting a chance to choose their time: Breast cancer patients say court overlooked them on assisted suicide." (Jane Gross)

Focuses on a breast cancer support group, and their discussion of the Supreme Court ruling that there is no fundamental right to assisted suicide, leaving states the right to ban the practice. Group favored a choice in this issue, comparing it to abortion.

June 30. "Cries of the dying awaken doctors to a new approach, palliative care." (Sheryl Gay Stolberg)

Discusses the palliative care approach to managing death. Article discusses the medical crisis of how to care for patients at the end of life, and how the assisted suicide debate has put new demands on the health care profession. Investigates the roots and philosophy behind palliative care, and practical problems of how to fit it into the modern health care system.

June 29. "Nine votes for judicial restraint: The Court rejects a 'right to die'—and the legacy of Roe v. Wade." (Jeffrey Rosen)

Reports on Supreme Court decision stating that there is no constitutional right to "doctor-assisted suicide," and hence passing the issue along to state legislatures. Decision reflects new concern for judicial restraint, although there is disagreement over the power of the court to grant constitutional exemptions in future.

June 29. "The good death: Embracing a right to die well." (Sheryl Gay Stolberg)

Begins with a discussion of what constitutes a "good death" in the wake of the Supreme Court ruling on "assisted suicide." Discusses the cultural taboos around discussing dying, and investigates what it really means to have a "good death."

June 29. "Letting the public decide about assisted suicide: The Court couldn't duck abortion and contraception forever. This moral issue, too, will be back." (David J. Garrow)

Reaction to the Supreme Court decision that there is no constitutional right to "physician-assisted suicide." Characterizes the Court as hoping to move the battleground for this issue to state legislatures, although further constitutional cases are expected from assisted suicide proponents.

June 28. "Two days that shaped the law." (Anon.; editorial on four key Supreme Court decisions, including the assisted-suicide decision. Stresses continuing debate on the issue.)

Discusses the U.S. Supreme Court decision on "physician-assisted suicide." Perfunctory report on the Court's decision to leave this matter to individual state legislatures, although intimating a certain openness to the issue for specific cases.

June 28. "'Passive euthanasia' in hospitals is the norm, doctors say." (Gina Kolata)

Article suggests that "managed deaths" are now the norm in America, intimating that a kind of "passive euthanasia" is common practice. Article questions whether such passive euthanasia constitutes "assisted suicide," or whether it is simply relief from suffering. Also discusses the shrouded manner in which physicians speak with their patients about the realities of death in our culture, and how we need to work harder at managing death.

June 28. "Woman's kin hires Kevorkian lawyer." (Anon.)

Family of woman who died under suspicious circumstances hires Kevorkian's lawyer, casting themselves into further question.

June 27. "Court, 9-0, upholds state laws prohibiting assisted suicide: No help for dying." (Linda Greenhouse. It is noteworthy that this is the main front-page story and is accompanied by other articles and excerpts from the Supreme Court's unanimous decisions.)

Report on U.S. Supreme Court decision that ruled that individual states may ban "doctor-assisted suicide," while leaving the door open for the Court to rule (constitutional exemptions) on specific cases in future. Discusses responses of individual judges, history of the case and possible public responses.

June 27. "From emotional to intellectual, secular to religious." (David Stout)

Report on reactions to the Supreme Court decision on assisted suicide, acknowledging that many of the difficult questions still remain unanswered. Reports on various reactions from religious and secular groups.

June 27. "Excerpts from court's decision upholding bans on assisted suicide." (Anon.)

Provides excerpts from American Supreme Court decision.

June 27. "Group proposes a new system on liver transplant priorities." (Gina Kolata)

Reports on new system for allocating organs for liver transplants to those who are most likely to survive as opposed to those sickest. Outlines rationale for new system, while conceding that it has its detractors.

June 27. "Handling of assisted-suicide cases unlikely to shift, officials say." (Esther B. Fein)

Despite legal prohibitions against "assisted suicide," this article claims that the practice is not uncommon, with the law appearing to take a noninterventionist stance regarding the problem. Reluctance to prosecute cases leaves them largely "moot."

June 27. "An issue that won't die: Court's ruling on doctor-assisted suicide leaves some basic questions unresolved." (Janny Scott)

Discusses the issues that remain unresolved in the wake of the Supreme Court decision, how decision will affect state legislatures, and the medical community, which needs to develop new responses to the issues of death and dying along with variety of responses (legal and medical).

June 27. "2 with intimate knowledge of how to look at death." (Neil A. Lewis)

Reports on the personal stake that judicial figures might have in deciding the assisted-suicide issue. Acknowledges how personal lives play into judicial decision making, arguing judicial impartiality is a myth.

June 24. "Anguished debate: Should doctors help their patients die?" (Anon.)

Excerpts from Herbert Hendin of the American Foundation for Suicide Prevention's article from *The Journal of the American Medical Association*, discussing problems with Dutch practices of physician-assisted suicide, and from Marcia Angell's article in the *New England Journal of Medicine*, arguing that traditional arguments against the legalization of assisted suicide are unpersuasive.

June 24. "Ethicists struggle against the tyranny of the anecdote." (Gina Kolata)

Tells of horror stories surrounding "assisted suicide" debate, and difficulty of resolving this issue.

June 23. "Doctors design rules on care for the dying." (Anon.)

Discusses guidelines released by the American Medical Association (which is opposed to doctor-assisted suicide) crafted to help people die with dignity. Provides an attempt to address end-of-life issues without sanctioning assisted suicide.

June 18. "Personal health: When a dying patient seeks suicide aid, it may be a signal to fight depression." (Jane E. Brody)

Argues that before honoring demands for assisted deaths, doctors should investigate whether patients are suffering from depression, and whether this ailment is impeding their ability to make clear decisions. Article questions whether death can be managed emotionally such that individuals would not request assisted suicide with present frequency. Depression is presented as an unnecessary, but manageable side effect of dying.

June 17. "Assisted-suicide guidelines encourage abuse." (Anon.)

Editorial letter from Hendin claims that guidelines for "physician-assisted suicide" actually lead to abuse and that the drafting of these guidelines for an illegal practice seems to sanction the same.

June 17. "Oregon braces for new right-to-die fight." (Carey Goldberg)

Report on Oregon's voters' facing a new vote on whether they want to repeal a law decreeing that terminally ill patients can ask their doctors for a prescription to end their lives. Discusses said law and opinions of its supporters and detractors.

June 15. "The nation: Suddenly, the new politics of morality." (Richard L. Berke)

Discusses how morality and politics are becoming increasingly intertwined as moral matters are brought into the political and legal forum. Considers the impact of such moral dilemmas on party politics.

June 14. "Beliefs: The Justices of the Supreme Court, preparing landmark opinions, are now writing about doctor-assisted suicide. They're hardly alone." (Peter Steinfels)

Outlines that there are myriad ethical, religious and philosophical concerns surrounding "assisted suicide" that will remain open for debate for much time to come, as evidenced by a plethora of publications up for release discussing the issue. Provides summer reading list on "euthanasia and assisted suicide."

June 13. "Mistrial declared in Kevorkian case after lawyer's statement." (Anon.)

Report of mistrial being declared in Kevorkian trial for "assisted suicide." Salutary report on court proceedings.

June 11. "Considering the unthinkable: Protocol for assisted suicide." (Sheryl Gay Stolberg)

Article discusses prevalence of "doctor-assisted suicide" within the medical community, despite illegalities. Discusses difficulties for groups writing guidelines and coming together to discuss issue that remains an underground, if not uncommon, practice.

June 10. "Oregon moves nearer to new vote on allowing assisted suicide." (Carey Goldberg)

Discusses how the right-to-die issue is being sent to Oregon voters. Balanced report on where certain groups stand on the issue and the arguments for their respective positions.

June 5. "Not enough is done to ease end of life, panel says." (Warren E. Leary)

Report on inadequacy of medicine's abilities to deal with end-of-life treatment. One commentator in the article suggests that the modern preoccupation with assisted suicide is a backlash against the medical community's inability to manage death, and patient fear that their end-of-life experiences will be painful and frightening.

June 4. "It's young vs. old in Germany as the welfare state fades." (Alan Cowell)

Discusses German problem of how to allocate resources to an aging population, and the inability of the young to carry the responsibility for these individuals and the pension system. No mention of assisted suicide.

May 30. "2 'perfect little girls' stun France in suicide." (Roger Cohen)

Tells of two French teenagers who commit a copycat suicide after popular music idol, Kurt Cobain.

May 4. "A better quality of life, in the days before death." (Esther B. Fein)

New York hospitals receive an injection of funds to aid them in improving the emotional and physical care of patients at the end of life. Reflects changing strategies in health care and managing the end of life.

April 18. "Nordic study links dementia to drivers in fatal crashes." (Denise Grady)

Scandinavian study suggests that there is a high incidence of early Alzheimer's in car crash victims over the age of 65. This is a serious consideration in light of an aging population. Study suggests that the preliminary stages of the disease could be a "significant traffic hazard."

April 10. "Kevorkian lawyer tied to suicide in Michigan." (Anon.)

Brief report of body of a young woman suffering from AIDS found in Michigan hotel room and linked to Dr. Jack Kevorkian.

April 5. "Beliefs: The issue of doctor-assisted suicide is put on the scales of justice, and philosophers weigh in." (Peter Steinfels; article on Dworkin et al., 1997)

Discusses the entry of philosophers into the debate on "assisted suicide" as they submit a brief to the Supreme Court in light of the upcoming ruling on "assisted suicide." The *Philosopher's Brief* suggests that individuals must be free to follow their own convictions with only the most minimal government interference, focusing on individual autonomy and the neutrality of the State. The article notes that philosophers, too, have their biases and that their position is rooted in a larger philosophical tradition.

April 5. "Stop aid, state tells Kevorkian." (Anon.)

Michigan state delivers a document to Kevorkian warning him to stop helping people commit suicide—which he publicly destroys. Kevorkian and the state continue to be at odds, although he remains unconvicted of any crime.

March 25. "Australia strikes down a state suicide law." (Anon.)

Brief report that Australia has struck down the world's only law allowing "doctor-assisted suicide" in favor of trying to improve pain management for the dying.

March 18. "H.M.O.s limiting medicare appeals, U.S. inquiry finds: Government is told by court to clarify its guidelines on elderly patients' rights." (Robert Pear)

Investigators suggest that H.M.O.s are limiting the options available to patients, and hence their decision-making abilities regarding medical treatment. There is a special concern for how this impacts the elderly. Basic, informative report on the health care industry and its economic considerations.

March 17. "Kevorkian is also painter. His main theme is death." (Keith Bradsher)

Illustrated article on "assisted suicide" doctor Kevorkian's art, exhibited in Michigan gallery. Paintings are said to reveal a dark and disturbing side of the "humanitarian" doctor.

March 13. "When a healer is asked, 'help me die.'" (Elizabeth Rosenthal)

Discusses doctor's views and experience with assisted suicide. Points to how doctors are divided on this issue, and discrepancies between the public opinions and those of medical organizations and practicing doctors. The article presents widely different views of various doctors, who collectively appear quite confused and torn about the issue.

March 8. "Kevorkian lawyer gives rationale for a suicide." (Anon.)

Brief report on release of statement by Kevorkian's lawyer detailing the rationale behind the latest assisted suicide associated with his client.

February 28. "Suicide law withstands a challenge." (Anon.)

Federal Courts reject a lawsuit challenging the Oregon law that is the first to allow "physician-assisted suicide" for terminally ill patients.

February 4. "Kevorkian is silent on 2 more deaths." (Anon.)

Brief report on the discovery of the bodies of two women having died of lethal injection in Michigan. Kevorkian has not acknowledged any involvement with the deaths.

February 2. "Assisted suicide: Australia faces a grim reality." (Seth Mydans)

Tells of the first patient to die under Australia's "voluntary euthanasia" law, the history of the law, its supporters and detractors. Also provides schematic on international status of the issue.

January 31. "The suicidal still call out in desperation." (Clyde Haberman)

Opinion piece suggests that "legally sanctioned death is on a roll," referring to the abortion and "assisted suicide" issues. Author argues we should shift energies to making the end of life more comfortable.

January 15. "Living wills aside, dying cling to hope." (Gina Kolata)

Author refers to a new comprehensive study on death and dying, and some of its findings. She suggests that faced with death, patients often do seek technologically advanced care, and will go to extreme lengths to prolong life. She points to the gap between "what healthy people think the seriously ill would want" and what is the reality for those suffering. Also raises questions about the nature of "terminal."

January 13. "How we die is our business." (Sherwin B. Nuland)

Opinion piece suggests that the irrationality of death has been overlooked in debates on "assisted suicide." Argues for the very individual logic of these decisions. Suggests that we turn inward to face the fears that color our decision making, and that this would reveal the real problem behind the assisted-suicide debate, which is the medical profession's reluctance to consider the comfort of the dying.

January 11. "Perspective: Doctor-assisted suicide." (Peter Steinfels)

Author speculates on upcoming U.S. Supreme Court ruling on constitutionality of assisted suicide, suggesting that regardless of the court decision, this issue will not go away. Also addresses some of the attenuating issues and implications of the assisted-suicide debate. Article outlines the complexity of the issue and some of the often overlooked considerations attached to the debate.

January 9. "High court hears 2 cases involving assisted suicide. Justices, in an unusually personal session, reveal their reluctance to intercede." (Linda Greenhouse)

Report on upcoming U.S. Supreme Court decisions surrounding assisted suicide suggests that the judiciary seems fascinated by the issue, and yet determined to keep out of such large life and death questions.

January 9. "New York's chief lawyer argues suicide case." (Dan Barry)

Report on the appearance of the attorney generals of New York and Washington before the U.S. Supreme Court to voice opposition to physician-assisted suicide, and the dramatic differences in their approaches, focusing on the drama of the New York lawyer's statement.

January 6. "Assisted suicide and the law." (Anon.)

Discusses upcoming debate moving to U.S. Supreme Court. Discusses the issues and the opinions of people on both sides of the debate. There is acknowledgment that assisted suicide is a not uncommon practice, but a suggestion that it needs to be brought out into the light.

January 6. "Court denies Kevorkian has a right to aid suicide." (Anon.)

Federal Court judge in Michigan denies that there is a constitutional right to "physician-assisted suicide." Kevorkian was attempting to prove that the "common law" against assisted suicide was unconstitutional.

January 5. "Before the court, the sanctity of life and death." (Anon.; includes disturbing comparative photographs of Mary Bowen Hall)

Article provides excerpts from briefs submitted for consideration during the U.S. Supreme Court's consideration of the constitutional question of assisted suicide. Excerpts are from a wide variety of sources and consider numerous facets of the issue. The article is accompanied by disturbing comparative photographs of cancer patient Mary Bowen Hall, one of the plaintiffs in the Supreme Court case.

January 1. "Alzheimer patients present a lesson on human dignity." (Gina Kolata)

Alzheimer's patients recount what it is like to live with the disease, providing a voice for sufferers of an illness that often robs patients of their ability to speak credibly in the public forum. Powerful story humanizes Alzheimer's sufferers and provides compelling anecdotal evidence of what it is like to suffer from the disease.

January 1. "Doctor at center of Supreme Court case on assisted suicide." (Jane Gross)

Report on Dr. Timothy Quill and his stance on "assisted suicide." Provides an analysis and discussion of the issue, its proponents, detractors and legal status. Quill suggests that aiding in dying is a last step in a doctor-patient relationship. Quill argues that the medical profession is ignoring the issue to their detriment and to the detriment of their patients.

1996

December 27. "Missouri drops an assisted-suicide case." (Anon.)

Charges of "assisted suicide" are dropped against family members of terminally ill Illinois woman.

November 25. "Prosecutor goes against tide, going after Kevorkian." (Jack Lessenberry)

Report on Michigan prosecutor's decision to prosecute Kevorkian despite precedents indicating the Court's reluctance to convict Kevorkian of assisting suicide.

November 24. "Slippery slope: A psychiatrist looks at physician-assisted suicide and shudders." (Charles E. Rosenberg; *Book Review* section)

Review of book by Herbert Hendin discussing the Dutch experience surrounding "assisted suicide," wherein he presents the Dutch as having moved along the slippery slope to a "euthanasia" that is suffering from grievous abuses. Psychiatrist Hendin argues against assisted suicide in light of this, although the reviewer is skeptical as to the effectiveness of Hendin's argument.

November 15. "In shift, prospects for survival will decide liver transplants." (Gina Kolata)

Report on new system for allocating organs for liver transplants to those who are most likely to survive as opposed to those sickest.

November 13. "Dying Cardinal lobbies against suicide aid." (Gustav Niebuhr)

Ailing Cardinal writes personal letter to U.S. Supreme Court justices encouraging them to deny a constitutional right to assisted suicide, based on his own end-of-life experiences and fears that such a right would be subject to abuses. Cardinal writes from a theological perspective arguing for the protection of traditional religious and cultural beliefs in the sanctity of life.

November 7. "Kevorkian is arrested and charged in a suicide." (Jack Lessenberry)

Reports Kevorkian's arrest, and charges laid against him, including helping a woman commit suicide. Kevorkian acknowledges being complicit in the "assisted suicide" of the woman involved in his charges, but appears nonplused, having been charged several times before but never convicted.

November 1. "Kevorkian indicted on charges of helping in three suicides." (Jack Lessenberry)

Kevorkian charged for "assisting suicide" in cases involving three women. Article indicates that Michiganers support Kevorkian, and that it is unlikely that he will be convicted of the charges.

October 18. "Another body left at hospital by Kevorkian." (Anon.)

Another brief account of a Kevorkian-assisted suicidist's body typically being left at a hospital.

October 14. "Therapy studied for survival rates: Resuscitated elderly patients did not make it home, Houston study finds." (Anon.)

Report on study finding low survival rate for elderly patients having received resuscitation. Claims elderly patients should be informed of diminished survival rates so that patients and physicians can make more informed decisions about resuscitation options.

October 6. "An issue for a reluctant court." (Linda Greenhouse)

The United States Supreme Court announces it will rule on questions surrounding "physician-assisted suicide," despite its reticence to speak to this issue. The Court is represented as being characteristically conservative about dealing with such hot social issues.

October 2. "High Court to say if the dying have a right to suicide help." (Linda Greenhouse)

Report on Supreme Court agreement to rule on whether the Constitution gives terminally ill patients a right to a doctor's assistance in hastening death. The debate focuses on the difference between assisting suicide and allowing patients to die. Arguments on both sides of the debate are presented, although with perhaps slightly more favorable treatment of the pro side.

September 26. "Australian man first in world to die with legal euthanasia." (Anon.)

Report on the first person to die under the world's first law permitting "voluntary euthanasia."

September 26. "A husband defends his decision to kill his wife." (Walter Goodman)

Reports on upcoming *Dateline* television show on man who helped his wife die because she was suffering from a degenerative disease. Focus is on whether wife consented to the death, other family members claiming that it would have been against the woman's wishes. Article suggests that the man's story is less than convincing, but does not present an unfavorable picture of the practice of assisted suicide generally.

August 29. "Dr. Kevorkian runs wild." (Timothy Quill and Betty Rolin)

Argues that there should be parameters and guidelines for physicians practicing doctor-assisted suicide, and that Kevorkian's own practices indicate neglect of any concern for the same. Argues against Kevorkian's maverick tactics and urges the public to focus instead on asserting the need for government regulation of the practice.

August 20. "Clash in Detroit over how ill a Kevorkian client really was."

Medical examiner questions whether Kevorkian patient was suffering to the extent Kevorkian alleges, claiming evidence indicates that the patient was obese and depressed, but not as ailing as Kevorkian argues. Various factors in this particular case point to the difficult nature of assessing whether a patient is "ready to die," and what factors should be considered in validating consent.

August 18. "Question of family violence arises in a Kevorkian suicide case." (Anon.)

Report on the history of family violence in the case of one patient who committed suicide with the aid of Kevorkian, and how this might have impacted her ability to consent to her death. Kevorkian claims not to have known of this aspect of his patient's history.

August 14. "When savings run out, some shun lifesaving." (Susan Gilbert)

Reports on study indicating that ill patients may forgo intensive life-prolonging treatments because they lack the financial resources to pursue such care. Patients might forgo treatment for fear of depleting life savings, and diminishing the future quality of life for their loved ones. Study indicates that these considerations might be playing out behind closed doors, leaving

physicians unaware of the role of patient's financial considerations in their end-of-life decisions.

July 21. "The next pro-lifers." (Paul Wilkes; *Magazine* section)

Preceding a Washington anti-assisted-suicide conference, planned to strategize for an upcoming Supreme Court case, the author discusses the issues with assisted-suicide detractors,
finding that many of their objections are not overzealous and
not easily dismissed. He examines the issue from religious,
medical, legal and ethical perspectives, providing a comprehensive article on the opponents of assisted suicide.

July 21. "Rush to lethal judgment." (Stephen L. Carter; *Magazine* section)

Article suggests that, increasingly, we do not believe that our
lives belong to us alone. Author says that there are certain difficulties in attempting to answer the assisted-suicide debate
through constitutional channels, citing problems with the handling of the matter in recent court cases. He claims that sometimes the courts are not the best place to solve ethical
difficulties.

July 15. "Many turning to Internet for aid with suicide." (Jack Lessenberry)

Report on the efficacy of the Internet in disseminating information about assisted suicide. The Internet has been a useful forum
for individuals to speak of an otherwise taboo subject, and en-
thusiastic response indicates public interest and concern with
this subject.

July 15. "The doctor's call." (M. Cathleen Kaveny and John P. Langan)

Report on American Medical Association's recent vote upholding its position of opposition to physician-assisted suicide.
Argues that physicians may have a unique perspective for appreciating the ills of, or risks associated with, assisted suicide, and
that the public should listen to their reservations.

June 26. "A.M.A. keeps its policy against aiding suicide." (Anon.)

Brief report on American Medical Association's vote to uphold
its position against doctor-assisted suicide.

June 12. "Kevorkian assists woman from New Jersey in dying." (Anon.)

Report on Kevorkian's latest incidence of assisting a patient to die, following his legal acquittal of charges of assisting suicide. Details the woman's medical condition and Kevorkian's legal history to this point.

May 23. "1 in 5 nurses tell survey they helped patients die." (Gina Kolata)

Report on study indicating that 20 percent of nurses have helped patients die, while also questioning statistical credibility of this survey, indicating the delicacy with which questions surrounding this issue need to be framed in order to be meaningful. Discusses difficulty, even among health care providers, in assessing whether certain situations should actually qualify as euthanasia. Reports involvement of nurses, not just physicians, in end-of-life issues.

May 18. "Man who helped wife die to serve 6 months." (Gary Pierre-Pierre)

Report of convicted of man who "helped his wife commit suicide." A large part of the issue centers on whether the death was consensual or coerced.

May 15. "Jury acquits Kevorkian in common-law case." (Jack Lessenberry)

Kevorkian acquitted in charges of violating a common law against "assisted suicide." Charge was particularly difficult to uphold because of the contentious existence of the so-called "common law."

May 14. "Dr. Kevorkian on trial, with hints of the future." (Carey James)

Report on *Frontline* television report on Kevorkian, his trial and his campaign for the legalization of "assisted suicide." The program is presented as primarily a biography on Kevorkian, rather than an intelligent discussion of "assisted suicide" and its attendant issues.

May 10. "Kevorkian back at trial as talk of Detroit is of another suicide." (Anon.)

Report on Kevorkian's "assisted suicide" trial. This case differs from others in that there were doctors attendant at the death, and "patholysis," Kevorkian's term for "doctor-assisted suicide," was printed on the death certificate.

May 9. "Tape recalls a Canadian's gratitude to Kevorkian." (Clyde H. Farnsworth)

Canadian leaves behind tape thanking Kevorkian for assisting in his suicide, and criticizing the Canadian government for having left him no recourse than to seek Kevorkian's help in facilitating death, having spent the past two years of his life campaigning for the legalization of "assisted suicide." Article is somewhat critical of the Canadian government for not directly addressing the "assisted suicide" issue.

May 7. "Kevorkian repeatedly disrupts his trial, calling it a lynching." (Jack Lessenberry)

Report on Kevorkian trial and Kevorkian's own indignant theatrics in court. Kevorkian is not pictured particularly favorably, but there is also not a strong feeling that the charge is within the bounds of the law.

May 5. "Appeals set back Kevorkian trial repeatedly." (Anon.)

Report on the sensationalistic and theatrical setbacks that are commonplace at the Kevorkian trials, wherein he is charged with "assisting suicide." Describes videotapes of the women Kevorkian is alleged to have helped commit suicide, and their testimonies that their deaths were consensual and desired. Not unfavorable treatment of the issue.

April 23. "Specialist testifies depression was issue in Kevorkian cases." (Jack Lessenberry)

Specialist testifying at Kevorkian trial suggests that Kevorkian patients might not have wished to die had they been treated for clinical depression, and that Kevorkian was remiss for not insisting that patients receive such treatment before validating their consent. Victim's families denied that their loved one's were clinically depressed despite their obvious sufferings.

April 7. "The Justices' life-or-death choices." (David J. Garrow)

New York Federal Courts strike down a 19th-century law against aiding or abetting suicide, putting the question of a right to a "physician-accelerated death" into the public forum. Article draws parallels between this issue and the abortion and capital punishment issues. Points to the persistent and pressing nature of assisted suicide as a public issue.

April 4. "Suicide ruling raises concern: Who decides?" (James Dao)

The New York Court strikes down a state ban on "physician-assisted suicide," raising questions of how the legislature should respond to the issue. Refers to a 1994 task force on this issue and the problems it encountered, leading to a continued persistence of ban. Discusses potential guidelines that would have to be incorporated into a law, and reluctance on the part of some to sanction the practice legally at all.

April 3. "Court overturns ban in New York on aided suicides: A historic shift, federal ruling allows doctors to prescribe drugs to end life." (Frank Bruni)

Describes case wherein New York Federal Court strikes down a state ban on "assisted suicide." Discusses status of assisted-suicide laws in other states, including Washington, where prohibitions have also been lifted. Acknowledges that laws against assisted suicide do not prevent its occurrence. Debate focuses around slippery slope issues, particularly regarding potential abuses of laws, and the issue of choice to die with dignity.

April 3. "Court overturns ban in New York on aided suicides: The decision offers relief to plaintiffs." (Esther B. Fein)

Acknowledges that assisted suicide is not an uncommon practice in the medical community, despite illegalities. Doctors, including Quill, discuss their decisions to engage in the practice.

March 31. "Right to die: Life after Quinlan." (Jeff Stryker)

Looks back at Quinlan decision, which allowed the right to forgo life-sustaining treatment, telling of the impact this case has had on the medical community and the right-to-die movement. Tells of upcoming cases medically similar to Quinlan's, and their unknown outcomes. Also touches on how the "assisted suicide" debate impacts this issue.

1995

July 2. "Live and let die: A doctor's best hopes can be a patient's worst nightmare." (Harriet Brickman)

Author discusses her own family's experiences with their decision not to prolong the life of her ailing father. She attributes her family's relative ease in facilitating their father's wishes to their physician's awareness of their father's views and a show of un-wavering public solidarity on the part of the family.

May 7. "We all must die; who can tell us when?" (Daniel J. Kevles; *Book Review* section)

Review of Peter Singer's book, which raises questions of person-hood, demanding a more coherent ethics of life and death. Singer argues that "euthanasia" and "assisted suicide" should be made legally available. Also reviews Herbert Hendin's book on suicide, focusing on his "euthanasia" chapter, which argues not against euthanasia, but that each case needs to be handled individually by trained professionals. Hendin also raises slippery slope issues.

April 25. "Justices declines to hear appeals involving assisted suicide." (Linda Greenhouse)

The author reports on the seeming reluctance of the U.S. Su-preme Court to address appeals on issues of whether there is a constitutional right to assisted suicide, and whether someone who helps another person commit suicide can be prosecuted for murder. One challenge was presented by Kevorkian, perhaps contributing to the Court reluctance to become involved in this publicly controversial issue.

March 5. "Hush of suicide." (Jennifer Farbar; *Magazine* section)

Author discusses her father's suicide, and the taboos associated with suicide in our culture, arguing that the subject needs to be more open to social discussion. She calls for "humane and real-istic" discussion of euthanasia and suicide, which would allow for greater information regarding choices surrounding the same.

1994

May 7. "When is it right to die?" (Ronald Dworkin)

Refers to Washington State Federal Court decision that laws against "assisted suicide" were unconstitutional, making "eutha-nasia" and assisted suicide difficult issues to ignore in legal and political forums. Author argues against slippery slope argu-ments, claiming that legislators have the ability to put effective safeguards into place. This opinion piece argues for the humane nature of euthanasia, and demands that arguments surrounding the sanctity of life consider also quality of life and dying with dignity.

1991

December 15. "A cosmological event." (Timothy Ferris; *Magazine* section)

Speculative piece about the nature of death. Examines phenomenon of near-death experiences, searching for (primarily biological) roots of the phenomenon.

December 8. "A fight to the death." (Trip Gabriel)

Discusses recently published *Final Exit*, and the personal history of its author in the wake of his ex-wife's own suicide. Salacious account outlines the woman's voiced reservations about the right to die and "euthanasia," despite her previous membership in the Hemlock Society.

December 1. "Hospitals will now ask patients if they wish to make death plan." (Lisa Belkin)

Report on New Jersey law, requiring admitted hospital patients to be presented with option to complete advanced directives regarding death and attendant ethical issues. Discusses history leading to creation of the law, and its positive impact in spurning discussion about death and dying.

August 18. "In matters of life and death, the dying take control." (Elizabeth Rosenthal)

Article argues population wants to take more control over end-of-life issues, citing recent developments including the publication of *Final Exit*, and the influence of Kevorkian and Quill. Discusses arguments from supporters and detractors of the issue in light of economics, an aging population and advancing medical technology. Balanced discussion of an up-and-coming issue.

August 9. "How-to book on suicide surges to top of best-seller list in week." (Lawrence Altman)

Discusses the success of Derek Humphry's *Final Exit*, and public responses to the publication, as an indication of how concern with "euthanasia" issue is rising.

July 7. "The life left behind." (Lee Anne Schreiber)

Not entirely favorable review of a book detailing a daughter's attempt to come to terms with her mother's suicide.

April 14. "They rarely leave a note." (Dava Sobel; *Book Review* section)

Favorable review of *The Enigma of Suicide*, book focusing on youth and adult suicides.

1990

December 23. "What medical science can't seem to learn: When to call it quits." (Andrew Malcolm)

Discusses two court cases on end-of-life issues, and when to terminate life. Anticipates "heated debates" on this front, documenting increasing support of "euthanasia," despite a general reluctance among the American public to discuss death.

August 26. "Programmed for life and death." (John Markoff)

Interest piece stemming from virtual-suicide of one techno-enthusiast discusses impact of computers on the way we live, work and die, through forging electronic communities.

1989

July 19. "When long life is too much: Suicide rises among elderly." (Martin Tolchin)

Report on study indicating that the suicide rate among the elderly has risen unusually during the 1980's. Suggests quality of life issues may be affecting decision of elderly to take their own lives as an increasing number of people perceive "rational suicide" as a solution to end-of-life discomforts.

June 25. "Body and mind: The loss of a self." (Melvin Konner, M.D.; *Magazine* section)

Piece provides anecdotal evidence on problems of Alzheimer's disease. Author demands the medical community address the physiological and emotional problems for those coping with the disease, as physicians struggle to alleviate a problem that cannot "fix." Raises quality of life questions as we find the body outliving the brain.

June 4. "Body and mind: What is too old?" (Michael S. Wilkes, M.D. and Mirian Shuchman, M.D.; *Magazine* section)

Argues that doctors may be neglecting care of elderly patients by denying them treatment options due to age discrimination. Discusses the need for special geriatric care for elderly (female) patients.

February 18. "Creating beauty out of suffering as life fades." (Douglas Martin)

Description of hospice care and one hospice's efforts to make life more enjoyable through a program that attends to the cosmetic and beauty needs of patients.

February 7. "For many, turmoil of aging erupts in the 50's, studies find." (Daniel Goleman)

Report on study identifying the 50's as decade where individuals begin to contemplate aging, discussing our cultural inability to respond to concerns about continuing quality of life and fears of death as one ages. Also describes difference in how men and women cope with aging.

1988

December 4. "Body and mind: Mortality." (Melvin Konner, M.D.; *Magazine* section)

Discussion of American cult of youth, and the related fears of aging in this society. Author opines that we require better cultural strategies for coping with aging.

November 10. "Personal health: An alert for older Americans about preventable adverse reactions to many common drugs." (Jane L. Brody)

Report on the unusual and potentially debilitating effects that certain prescription drugs can have on the elderly, while offering some explanations for the same.

November 5. "Before going into that good night." (John Houseman)

Excerpt from book by actor Houseman, telling of his personal feelings about aging and his gradual acceptance of the inevitability of death.

October 15. "Excerpts from the Court of Appeals decision on a patient's right to die." (Anon.)

Excerpts from the New York State Court of Appeals decision on the right of a patient to refuse life-sustaining treatment. The majority decision focuses on sanctity to life and need for explicit instructions in cases where one wishes to forgo life sustaining treatment, while the dissent argues that the patient has indeed sufficiently expressed her wishes.

October 15. "New York's highest court rejects family's plea in right-to-die case." (E. R. Shipp)

Reports on New York Court decision on "right to die" case, ruling that an elderly woman must be kept alive through artificial feeding despite the family's insistence that the woman would prefer to die. Case is marked as first of its kind where the Court has decided against "patient autonomy."

October 15. "Many courts have upheld right to die." (E. R. Shipp)

In the wake of New York Court decision, reports on previous Court decisions on "right to die" issue, noting that they have generally upheld the right to die.

1. My thanks to Karen Weteleinen, Ivana Dragicevic, Kajori Rahman and Jane Isaacs-Doyle, who contributed to compiling this annotated bibliography.

BIBLIOGRAPHY

Agee, James. 1985. *A Death in the Family*. New York: Bantam.

Alther, Lisa. 1976. *Kinflicks*. London: Penguin.

Alvarez, Al. 1971. *The Savage God: A Study of Suicide*. New York: Penguin.

Anders, George. 1997. *Health Against Wealth: HMOs and the Breakdown of Medical Trust*. New York: Houghton Mifflin.

Angell, Marcia. 1997. "Editorials: The Supreme Court and Physician-Assisted Suicide—The Ultimate Right." *New England Journal of Medicine*, 336(1): 50–53.

——. 1990. "The Right to Die in Dignity." *Newsweek*, 116(July 23, 1990): 9.

Aries, Phillipe. 1982. *The Hour of Our Death*. Trans. Helen Weaver. New York: Vintage Books.

Artaud, Antonin. 1995. "On Suicide." in *Le Disque Vert*, No. 1, 1925, quoted in *The Columbia Dictionary of Quotations*, 1995, New York: Columbia University Press, Microsoft *Bookshelf*, 1996–97 CD-ROM edition.

Baechler, Jean. 1975. *Suicides*. Trans. Barry Cooper. New York: Basic Books.

Battin, Margaret Pabst. 1996. *The Death Debate: Ethical Issues in Suicide*. Englewood Cliffs, N.J.: Prentice-Hall. (This is the same work as Battin, 1995, with a Foreword by Dr. Timothy Quill and repaginated.)

——. 1995. *Ethical Issues in Suicide*. Englewood Cliffs, N.J.: Prentice-Hall. (Revised version of Battin, 1982b.)

——. 1994. *The Least Worst Death: Essays in Bioethics on the End of Life*. New York: Oxford University Press.

——. 1992a. "Voluntary Euthanasia and the Risks of Abuse: Can We Learn Anything from the Netherlands?" *Law Medicine and Health Care*, 20(1–2): 133–143.

——. 1992b. "Assisted Suicide: Can We Learn Anything from Germany?" *Hastings Center Report*, March–April, 44–51.

——. 1991. "Euthanasia: The Way We Do It, the Way They Do It." *Journal of Pain and Symptom Management*, 6(5): 298–305.

——. 1990. *Ethics in the Sanctuary: Examining the Practices of Organized Religion*. New Haven: Yale University Press.

——. 1987. "Choosing the Time to Die: The Ethics and Economics of Suicide in Old Age." Spicker, Ingman and Lawson, 1987.

——. 1982a. "The Concept of Rational Suicide." Shneidman, 1984: 297–320.

——. 1982b. *Ethical Issues in Suicide*. Englewood Cliffs, N.J.: Prentice-Hall.

Battin, Margaret Pabst, and Arthur G. Lipman, 1996. *Drug Use in Assisted Suicide and Euthanasia*. New York: Pharmaceutical Products Press.

Battin, Margaret Pabst, and D. J. Mayo, eds. 1980. *Suicide: The Philosophical Issues*. New York: St. Martin's.

Bayer, Ronald, Daniel Callahan, John Fletcher, et al. 1983. "The Care of the Terminally Ill: Morality and Economics." *New England Journal of Medicine*, 309: 1490–1494.

Baylis, Francoise, Jocelyn Downie, Benjamin Freedman, Barry Hoffmaster and Susan Sherwin, eds., 1995. *Health Care Ethics in Canada*. Toronto: Harcourt Brace.

Beauchamp, Tom L. 1996. *Intending Death: The Ethics of Assisted Suicide and Euthanasia*. Upper Saddle River, N.J.: Prentice-Hall.

——. 1980. "Suicide." Regan, 1980: 77.

——, ed. 1975. *Ethics and Public Policy*. Englewood Cliffs, N.J.: Prentice-Hall.

Beauchamp, Tom L., and James Childress. 1994. *Principles of Biomedical Ethics*, 4th edition. Oxford: Oxford University Press.

——. 1989. *Principles of Biomedical Ethics*, 3rd edition. Oxford: Oxford University Press.

——. 1979. *Principles of Biomedical Ethics*. New York and Oxford: Oxford University Press.

Beauchamp, Tom L., and LeRoy Walters. 1989. *Contemporary Issues in Bioethics*, 3rd edition. Belmont, Calif.: Wadsworth Publishing Company.

Beauchamp, Tom L., and Seymour Perlin, eds. 1978. *Ethical Issues in Death and Dying*. Englewood Cliffs, N.J.: Prentice-Hall.

Benjamin, Martin, and Joy Curtis. 1986. *Ethics in Nursing*. Oxford: Oxford University Press.

Bennahum, D., G. Kimsma, C. Spreeuwenberg, et al. 1993. "Been There: Physicians Speak for Themselves." *Cambridge Quarterly of Healthcare Ethics*, 2: 9–17.

Benrubi, Guy. 1992. "Euthanasia—The Need for Procedural Safeguards." *New England Journal of Medicine*, 326(3): 197–199.

Berger, David M. 1987. *Clinical Empathy*. Northvale: Aronson. Quoted in Code, 1994: 83.

Betzold, Michael. 1993. *Appointment with Dr. Death*. Troy, Mich.: Momentum Books.

Biggs, H., and K. Diesfeld. 1995. "Assisted Suicide for People with Depression: An Advocate's Perspective." *Medical Law International*, 2: 23–37.

Birren, James E. 1968. "Psychological Aspects of Aging: Intellectual Functioning." *The Gerontologist*, 8: 16–19.

Birren, James E., and K. Warner Schaie, eds. 1977. *Handbook of the Psychology of Aging*. New York: Van Nostrand.

Bloch, Sidney, and Paul Chodoff, eds. 1991. *Psychiatric Ethics*, 2nd edition. Oxford: Oxford University Press.

Blythe, Ronald. 1979. *The View in Winter*. New York: Harcourt Brace Jovanovich.

Bonsteel, Alan. 1997. "Behind the White Coat." *The Humanist*, March/April, 57(2): 15–18.

Brandt, R. B. 1975. "The Morality and Rationality of Suicide." Perlin, 1975: 61–75.

Bresnahan James F. 1993. "Medical Futility or the Denial of Death?" *Cambridge Quarterly of Healthcare Ethics*, 2(2): 213–217.

Brock, Dan. 1989. "Death and Dying." Veatch, 1989.

——. 1986. "Forgoing Life-Sustaining Food and Water: Is It Killing?" In Lynn, 1986.

Brodie, Howard. 1976. *Ethical Decisions in Medicine*. Boston: Little, Brown and Company.

Brody, H. 1992. "Assisted Death—A Compassionate Response to a Medical Failure." *New England Journal of Medicine*, 327(19): 1384–1388.

Brooks, Simon A. 1984. "Dignity and Cost-Effectiveness: A Rejection of the Utilitarian Approach to Death." *Journal of Medical Ethics*, 10: 148–151.

Brown, Judy. 1995. *The Choice: Seasons of Loss and Renewal After a Father's Decision to Die*. Berkeley: Conari Press.

Brown, Newell. 1986. *How Not to Overstay One's Life: To Call It a Day—In Good Season*. Nederland, Colo.: Privately published; available from Newell Brown, Twin Sisters Road, Magnolia Star Route, Nederland, Colo. 80466.

Buchanan, Alan. 1978. "Medical Paternalism." *Philosophy and Public Affairs* 7(1978): 370–390.

Burgess, J. A. 1993. "The Great Slippery-Slope Argument." *Journal of Medical Ethics*, 19: 169–174.

Caine, Eric. 1993. "Self-Determined Death, the Physician, and Medical Priorities: Is There Time to Talk?" *Journal of the American Medical Association*, 270(7): 875–876.

Callahan, Daniel. 1995. "When Self-Determination Runs Amok." In Baylis et al., 1995: 555–562.

———. 1993. "Pursuing a Peaceful Death." *Hastings Center Report*, 1993, 23(4): 33–38.

Callahan, Joan C. 1986. "Paternalism and Voluntariness." *Canadian Journal of Philosophy* 16: 2 (1986) 199–220.

Campbell, Robert, and Diane Collinson. 1988. *Ending Lives*. Oxford: Basil Blackwell, 1988.

Caplan, Arthur. 1981. "The 'Unnaturalness' of Aging—A Sickness Unto Death?" In Caplan et al., 1981: 725–737.

Caplan, Arthur, H. Tristram Engelhardt, Jr., and James J. McCartney, eds. 1981. *Concepts of Health and Disease*. Reading, Mass.: Addison-Wesley.

Capron, Alexander Morgan. 1992. "The Patient Self-Determination Act: A Cooperative Model for Implementation." *Cambridge Quarterly of Healthcare Ethics*, 1(2): 97–106.

———. 1986. "Legal and Ethical Problems in Decisions for Death." *Law, Medicine and Health Care*, 14(3–4): 141–144, 157.

Carpenter, B. 1993. "A Review and New Look at Ethical Suicide in Advanced Age." *The Gerontologist*, 33(3): 359–365.

Chappell P., and R. King. 1992. *"Final Exit* and the Risk of Suicide." *Journal of the American Medical Association* (Letters) 267(22): 3027.

Charlton R., S. Dovey, Y. Mizushima, and E. Ford. 1995. "Attitudes to Death and Dying in the UK, New Zealand, and Japan." *Journal of Palliative Care*, 11(1): 42–47.

Checkland, David, and Michel Silberfeld. 1996. "Mental Competence and the Question of Beneficent Intervention." *Theoretical Medicine*, 17(2): 121–134.

——. 1995. "Reflections on Segregating and Assessing Areas of Competence." *Theoretical Medicine*, 16: 375–388.

——. 1993. "Competence and the Three A's: Autonomy, Authenticity, and Aging." *Canadian Journal on Aging*, 12(4): 453–468.

Childress, James F. 1979. "Paternalism and Health Care." Robinson and Pritchart, 1979: 18.

Choron, Jacques. 1972. *Suicide*. New York: Scribners.

——. 1963. *Death and Western Thought*. London: Collier-Macmillan.

Ciesielski-Carlucci, C. 1993. "Physician Attitudes and Experiences with Assisted Suicide: Results of a Small Opinion Survey." *Cambridge Quarterly of Healthcare Ethics*, 2: 39–44.

Clark, Nina. 1997. *The Politics of Physician Assisted Suicide*. New York: Garland.

Code, Lorraine. 1994. "I Know Just How You Feel." More and Milligan, 1994: 77–97.

Colt, George Howe. 1991. *The Enigma of Suicide*. New York: Summit Books.

Conwell, Yeates, and Eric Caine. 1991. "Rational Suicide and the Right to Die—Reality and Myth." *New England Journal of Medicine*, 325(15): 1100–1103.

Cowley, Malcolm. 1982. *The View from Eighty*. London: Penguin.

Cox, Donald. 1993. *Hemlock's Cup: The Struggle for Death with Dignity*. Buffalo, N.Y.: Prometheus Books.

Crane, Diana. 1975. *The Sanctity of Social Life: Physicians' Treatment of Critically Ill Patients*. New York: Russell Sage Foundation.

Crisp, R. 1987. "A Good Death: Who Best to Bring It?" *Bioethics*, 1(1): 74–79.

Crowley, J. 1992. "To Be or Not to Be: Examining the Right to Die." *Journal of Legislation of Notre Dame Law School*, 18(2): 347–355.

Culver, Charles M., and Bernard Gert. 1990. "The Inadequacy of Incompetence." *Milbank Memorial Quarterly*, 68: 619–643.

Daube, David. 1972. "The Linguistics of Suicide." *Philosophy and Public Affairs*, 1: 387–437.

Davis, A., L. Phillips, T. Drought, et al. 1995. "Nurses' Attitudes Towards Active Euthanasia." *Nursing Outlook* 43(4): 174–179.

Davis, John W., Barry Hoffmaster, and Sarah Shorten, eds. *Contemporary Issues in Biomedical Ethics*. Clifton, N.J.: Humana Press.

Day, M. 1994. "An Act of Will." *Nursing Times*, 90(10): 14.

de Beauvoir, Simone. 1969. *A Very Easy Death*. Harmondsworth: Penguin Books.

De Spelder, Lynne Ann, and Albert Lee Strickland. 1992. *The Last Dance: Encountering Death and Dying*, 3rd edition. Mountain View, Calif.: Mayfield Publishing Company.

DeSimone, Cathleen. 1996. *Death on Demand: Physician-Assisted Suicide in the United States*. Buffalo: W. S. Hein.

Devettere, Raymond J. 1992. "Slippery Slopes and Moral Reasoning." *The Journal of Clinical Ethics*, 3(4): 297–301.

Diegner, Leslie F., and Jeffrey Sloan. 1992. "Decision-Making During Serious Illness: What Role Do Patients Really Want to Play?" *Clinical Epidemiology*, 45(9): 941–950.

Doerr, Edd. 1997. "Liberty and Death." *The Humanist*, March/ April, 57(2): 12–13.

Donnelly, John, ed. 1997. *Suicide: Right or Wrong?* Buffalo: Prometheus Press.

——. 1978. *Language, Metaphysics, and Death*. New York: Fordham University Press.

Downie, R. S. 1994. "Limiting Treatment at the End of Life." *VESS Newsletter*, January, 1994, 1–3.

Downing, A. B., ed. 1969. *Euthanasia and the Right to Death: The Case for Voluntary Euthanasia*. Atlantic Highlands, N.J.: Humanities Press.

du Boulay, Shirley. 1984. *Cicely Saunders, Founder of the Modern Hospice Movement*. London: Hodder and Stoughton.

Drane, J. M. 1985. "The Many Faces of Competency." *Hastings Center Report*, 15(2): 17–21.

Dresser, R. 1995. "Dworkin on Dementia." *Hastings Center Report*, 25(6): 32–38.

——. 1994. "Missing Persons: Legal Perceptions of Incompetent Patients." *Rutgers Law Review*, 609: 636–647.

Dresser, R., and P. J. Whitehouse. 1994. "The Incompetent Patient on the Slippery Slope." *Hastings Center Report*, 24(4): 6–12.

Drey, P., and J. Giszczak. 1992. "May I Author My Final Chapter? Assisted Suicide and Guidelines to Prevent Abuse." *Journal of Legislation of the Notre Dame Law School*, 18(2): 331–345.

Durkheim, Émile. 1897. *Suicide: A Study in Sociology*. Trans. J. A. Spaulding and G. Simpson, 1951. New York: The Free Press.

Dworkin, Gerald. 1972. "Paternalism." *The Monist* 56 (Jan. 1972).

Dworkin, Ronald, et al. 1997. "Assisted Suicide: The Philosophers' Brief." *The New York Review of Books*, March 27, 44(5): 41–47.

——. 1996. "Sex, Death, and the Courts." *The New York Review of Books*, August 8, 43(13): 44–50.

——. 1993. *Life's Dominion: An Argument About Abortion and Euthanasia*. London: Harper Collins.

Ellin, Joseph. 1981. "Comments on 'Paternalism in Health Care.'" Davis, Hoffmaster and Shorten, eds., 1981.

Elliot, C. 1991. "Competence as Accountability." *Journal of Clinical Ethics*, 2: 3.

Emanuel, Ezekiel, and Linda Emanuel. 1993. "Decisions at the End of Life Guided by Communities of Patients." *Hastings Center Report*, 1993, September–October, 6–14.

Engelhardt, Jr., H. T. 1986. *The Foundations of Bioethics*. New York: Oxford University Press.

Farber, Leslie H. 1969. "The Phenomenology of Suicide." Shneidman, 1969: 109–110.

Feifel, Herman, ed. 1977. *New Meanings of Death*. New York: McGraw-Hill.

Feinberg, Joel. 1973. *Social Philosophy*. Engelwood Cliffs, N.J.: Prentice-Hall.

Feldman, Fred. 1992. *Confrontations with the Reaper: A Philosophical Study of the Nature and Value of Death*. New York and Oxford: Oxford University Press.

"Final Report of the Netherlands State Commission on Euthanasia: An English Summary." 1987. Trans. anon. *Bioethics*, 1(2): 163–174.

Fletcher, J. 1989. "The Right to Choose When to Die." *Hemlock Quarterly*, January.

Foley, K. 1991. "The Relationship of Pain and Symptom Management to Patient Requests for Physician-Assisted Suicide." *Journal of Pain and Symptom Management*, 6(5): 289–297.

Freud, Sigmund. 1915. "Our Attitude Towards Death." Chapter 2, *Thoughts for the Times on War and Death. The Standard Edition of the Complete Works of Sigmund Freud*. London: Hogarth Press. Quoted in Battin, 1982: 318, n. 3.

Fulton, Robert, et al. 1976. *Death, Grief and Bereavement: A Bibliography, 1845–1975*. New York: Arno Press.

Garret, J., R. Harris, J. Norburn, D. Patrick, and M. Danis. 1993. "Life-Sustaining Treatments during Terminal Illness: Who Wants What?" *Journal of General Internal Medicine*, 8: 361–368.

Garrett, T. M., H. W. Baillie, and R.M. Garrett. 1988. *Health Care Ethics: Principles and Problems*. Englewood Cliffs, N.J.: Prentice-Hall.

Gay, Kathlyn. 1993. *The Right to Die: Public Controversy, Private Matter (Issue and Debate)*. Brookfield: Millbrook Press, Inc.

Gaylin, W., L. Kas, E. D. Pellegrino, and M. Siegler. 1988. "Doctors Must Not Kill." *Journal of the American Medical Association*, 259: 2139–2140.

Geis, Sally B., and Donald Messer. 1997. *How Shall We Die? Helping Christians Debate Assisted Suicide*. New York: Abingdon Press.

Gentles, Ian. 1995. *Euthanasia and Assisted Suicide: The Current Debate*. Toronto: Stoddart.

Genuis, Stephen J., et al. 1994. "Public Attitudes Toward the Right to Die." *Canadian Medical Association Journal*, 150(5): 701–708.

Gert, Bernard, and Charles M. Culver, "Paternalistic Behaviour." *Philosophy and Public Affairs*, 6 (1976).

Gillick, M., K. Hesse, and N. Mazzapica. 1993. "Medical Technology at the End of Life: What Would Physicians and

Nurses Want for Themselves?" *Archives of Internal Medicine*, 153: 2542–2547.

Graber, Glenn C. 1981. "On Paternalism in Health Care." Davis, Hoffmaster and Shorten, 1981.

Graber, Glenn C., and Jennifer Chassman. 1993. "Assisted Suicide Is Not Voluntary Active Euthanasia, But It's Awfully Close." *Journal of the American Geriatrics Society*, 41(1): 88–89.

Grollman, Earl A. 1970. *Talking About Death*. Boston: Beacon Press.

Gunnell, D., and S. Frankel. 1994. "Prevention of Suicide: Aspirations and Evidence." *British Medical Journal*, 308: 1227–1233.

Gustafson, J. M. 1993. "Commentary on 'Ain't Nobody Gonna Cut on My Head,'" in B. J. Crigger, ed., 1993, *Cases in Bioethics: Selections from the Hastings Center Report*. New York: St. Martin's Press, 199–200.

Gutmann, Stephanie. 1996. "Death and the Maiden." *The New Republic*, June 24, 20–21, 24, 28.

Hamel, Ronald, and Edwin DuBose, eds. 1996. *Must We Suffer Our Way to Death? Cultural and Theological Perspectives on Death by Choice*. Dallas: Southern Methodist University Press.

Hendin, Herbert. 1996. *Seduced by Death: Doctors, Patients, and the Dutch Cure*. New York: W. W. Norton.

Hinton, John. 1967. *Dying*. Harmondsworth, England: Penguin.

Hoefler, James. 1997. *Managing Death: The First Guide for Patients, Family Members, and Care Providers on Forgoing Treatment at the End of Life*. Boulder, Colo. and New York: Westview Press (Harper-Collins).

——. 1994. *Culture, Medicine, Politics, and the Right to Die*. Boulder, Colo. and Oxford: Westview Press.

Hook, Sidney. 1988. "The Uses of Death." *The New York Review of Books*, 25(7): 22–25.

Howe, Edmund G. 1992. "Caveats Regarding Slippery Slopes and Physicians' Moral Conscience." *The Journal of Clinical Ethics*, 3(4): 251–256.

Hume, David, 1826. "Essay on Suicide." (1776). In *The Philosophic Works of David Hume*. Edinburgh: Black and Tait. Quoted in Battin, 1982a: 312.

Hume, David, 1777 (1983). *An Enquiry Concerning the Principles of Morals*. Indianapolis: Hacket Publishing Co.

Humphry, Derek. 1994. "Suicide by Asphyxiation After the Publication of *Final Exit*." *New England Journal of Medicine* (Letters, Replies), 330(14): 1017.

——. 1993a. *Lawful Exit: The Limits of Freedom for Help in Dying*. Junction City, Oregon: Norris Lane Press.

——. 1993b. "Derek Humphry Discusses Death with Dignity with Thomasine Kushner." *Cambridge Quarterly of Healthcare Ethics*, 2(1): 57–61.

——. 1992a. *Final Exit: The Practicalities of Self-Deliverance and Assisted Suicide for the Dying*. New York: Dell.

——. 1992b. *Dying with Dignity*. New York: Birch Lane Press

——. 1992c. "The Last Choice." *Hemlock Quarterly*, October, 4.

Humphry, Derek, and A. Wickett. 1986. *The Right to Die—Understanding Euthanasia*. New York: Harper and Row. Reprinted, 1990, by the Hemlock Society, Eugene, Ore.

Hurley, S. L. 1989. *Natural Reasons: Personality and Polity*. New York: Oxford University Press.

Jamison, Stephen. 1996. *Final Acts of Love: Families, Friends, and Assisted Dying*. New York: The Putnam Publishing Group.

Johnston, Brian. 1994. *Death as a Salesman: What's Wrong with Assisted Suicide*. Sacramento: New Regency Publishing.

Judis, John B. 1997. "Careless: A Poison Pill for Medicare." *The New Republic*, July 28.

Kant, Immanuel. "Suicide." Thomas A. Mappes and Jane S. Zembaty. 1991. *Biomedical Ethics*, 3rd edition. New York: McGraw-Hill.

Kass, L. 1993. "Is There a Right to Die?" *Hastings Center Report*, January–February: 34–43.

Kastenbaum, Robert J. 1992. *The Psychology of Death*. New York: Springer Publishing Company.

——. 1991. *Death, Society, and Human Experience*. New York: Merrill.

——. 1967. "Suicide as the Preferred Way of Death." Shneidman, 1976.

——. 1964. *New Thoughts on Old Age*. New York: Springer.

Kastenbaum, Robert J., and Beatrice Kastenbaum, eds. 1989. *Encyclopedia of Death*. Phoenix: Oryx Press.

Kearl, Michael C. 1989. *Endings: A Sociology of Death and Dying*. New York: Oxford University Press.

Keizer, Bert. 1997. *Dancing with Mister D: Notes on Life and Death*. New York: Doubleday.

Kellogg, F., M. Crain, J. Corwin, and P. Brickner. 1992. "Life-Sustaining Interventions in Frail Elderly Persons—Talking About Choices." *Archives of Internal Medicine*, 152: 2317–2320.

Kluge, Eike-Henner. 1998. "The Treatment of Severely Disabled Newborns: Some Ethical Issues." Peter Singer and Helga Kuhse, eds., 1998, *The Oxford Companion to Bioethics*. New York: Oxford University Press.

——. 1994. "Ethics and Deliberate Death." *Last Rights*, 12: 23–43.

——. 1993. "Doctors, Death and Sue Rodriguez." *Canadian Medical Association Journal*, 148(6): 1015–1017.

———. 1992. *Biomedical Ethics in a Canadian Context*. Scarborough, Ont.: Prentice-Hall Canada Inc.

———. 1991a. "The Ethics of Forced Feeding in Anorexia Nervosa." *Canadian Medical Association Journal*, 144(9): 1121–1124.

———. 1991b. "Euthanasia and Related Taboos." *Canadian Medical Association Journal*, 144(3): 359–360.

———. 1981. *The Ethics of Deliberate Death*. Port Washington, N.Y. and London: Kennikat Press.

———. 1980. "The Euthanasia of Radically Defective Neonates: Some Statutory Considerations." *Dalhousie Law Journal*, 6(2): 229–257.

———. 1975. *The Practice of Death*. New Haven: Yale University Press.

Kluge, Eike-Henner, and Joseph E. Magnet. 1985. *Withholding Treatment from Defective Newborn Children*. Cowansville, Que.: Brown Legal Publications.

Kristol, Elizabeth. 1993. "Soothing Moral Shroud." *The Washington Post*, December 3.

Kübler-Ross, Elisabeth. 1969. *On Death and Dying*. New York: Macmillan.

Kung, Hans, and Walter Jens. 1995. *Dying with Dignity: A Plea for Personal Responsibility*. New York: Continuum.

Kushner, Howard. 1989. *Self-Destruction in the Promised Land*. New Brunswick: Rutgers University Press.

Ladd, John, ed. 1979. *Ethical Issues Relating to Life and Death*. New York: Oxford University Press.

Laurence, Margaret. 1964. *The Stone Angel*. Toronto: McClelland and Stewart.

Lee, M., and L. Ganzini. 1994. "The Effect of Recovery from Depression on Preferences for Life-Sustaining Therapy in Older Patients." *Journal of Gerontology*, 49(1): M15–M21.

Loewy, E. H. 1995. "Compassion, Reason, and Moral Judgement." *Cambridge Quarterly of Healthcare Ethics*, 4(4): 466–475.

——. 1991. *Suffering and the Beneficent Community*. Albany, N.Y.: SUNY Press.

Logue, Barbara. 1993. *Last Rights: Death Control and the Elderly in America*. Oxford: Maxwell Macmillan.

Lown, Bernard. 1997. *The Lost Art of Healing*. New York: Houghton Mifflin.

Lynn, Joanne, ed. 1986. *By No Extraordinary Means: The Choice to Forgo Life-Sustaining Food and Water*. Bloomington and Indianapolis: Indiana University Press.

Madigan, K. V., David Checkland, and Michel Silberfeld. 1994. "Presumptions Respecting Mental Competence." *Canadian Journal of Psychiatry*, 39(April): 147–151.

Maltsberger, John. 1994. "Calculated Risk-Taking in the Treatment of Suicidal Patients: Ethical and Legal Problems." *Death Studies*, 18: 439–452.

Maltsberger, John, and Mark Goldblatt, eds. 1996. *Essential Papers on Suicide*. New York: New York University Press.

Marcus, Eric. 1996. *Why Suicide: Answers to 200 of the Most Frequently Asked Questions About Suicide, Attempted Suicide, and Assisted Suicide*. San Francisco: Harper.

Martin, R. M. 1980. "Suicide and Self-Sacrifice." Battin and Mayo, 1980.

McGough, P. 1993. "Washington State Initiative 119: The First Public Vote on Legalizing Physician Assisted Death." *Cambridge Quarterly of Healthcare Ethics*, 2: 63–67.

McIntosh, John L., and Nancy J. Osgood. 1986. *Suicide and the Elderly*. Westport: Greenwood Press.

McLean, Sheila A. M., ed. 1996. *Death, Dying and the Law*. Brookfield, Vt.: Dartmouth Publishing Co.

Meier, D., and C. Cassel. 1983. "Euthanasia in Old Age—A Case Study and Ethical Analysis." *Journal of the American Geriatrics Society*, 31(5): 294–298.

Menninger, Karl. 1966. *Man Against Himself*. New York: A Harvest/HBJ Book.

Mezey, M., L. Evans, Z. Golub, E. Murphy, and G. White. 1994. "The Patient Self-Determination Act: Sources of Concern for Nurses." *Nursing Outlook*, 42(1): 30–38.

Mezey, M., and B. Latimer. 1993. "The Patient Self-Determination Act—An Early Look at Implementation." *Hastings Center Report*, January/February, 16–20.

Miles, S., and A. August. 1990. "Courts, Gender and the 'Right to Die.'" *Law, Medicine and Health Care*, 18: 85–95.

Mitford, Jessica. 1963. *The American Way of Death*. New York: Simon and Schuster.

Miyaji, N. T. 1993. "The Power of Compassion: Truth-Telling Among American Doctors in the Care of Dying Patients." *Social Science Medicine,* 36(3): 249–264.

Mullens, Anne. 1996. *Timely Death: Considering Our Last Rights*. New York: Alfred A. Knopf.

Narveson, Jan. 1986. "Moral Philosophy and Suicide." *Canadian Journal of Psychiatry*, 31: 104–107.

Nuland, Sherwin B. 1994. *How We Die: Reflections on Life's Final Chapter*. New York: Alfred A. Knopf.

Oates, Joyce Carol. 1980. "The Art of Suicide." Battin and Mayo, 1980: 161–168.

Ozar, David. 1992. "The Characteristics of a Valid 'Empirical' Slippery Slope Argument." *The Journal of Clinical Ethics*, 3(4): 301–302.

Pellegrino Edmund D. 1993. "Compassion Needs Reason Too." *Journal of the American Medical Association*, 270(7): 874–875.

——. 1992. "Doctors Must Not Kill." *The Journal of Clinical Ethics*, 3(2): 95–103.

Pepper-Smith, R., W. R. C. Harvey, Michel Silberfeld, E. Stein, and D. Rutman. 1992. "Consent to a Competency Assessment." *International Journal of Law and Psychiatry*, 15: 13–23.

Perlin, Seymour, ed. 1975. *A Handbook for the Study of Suicide*. Oxford: Oxford University Press.

Peruzzi, N., A. Canapary, and B. Bongar. 1996. "Physician-Assisted Suicide: The Role of Mental Health Professionals." *Ethics and Behaviour*, 6(4): 353–356.

Pohier, Jacques, and Dietmar Mieth. 1985. *Suicide and the Right to Die*. Edinburgh: T. and T. Clark, Ltd.

Powell, Tia, and Donald B. Kornfeld. 1993. "On Promoting Rational Treatment, Not Rational Suicide." *The Journal of Clinical Ethics*, 4(4): 334–335.

Prado, C. G. 1998. *The Last Choice: Preemptive Suicide in Advanced Age*, 2nd edition. New York and Westport, Conn.: Greenwood and Praeger Presses. (Extensively revised version of Prado, 1990.)

——. 1990. *The Last Choice: Preemptive Suicide in Advanced Age*. New York and Westport, Conn.: Greenwood Group.

Prado, C. G., and Taylor, S. J. 1999. *Assisted Suicide: Theory and Practice in Elective Death*. Amherst, N.Y.: Humanity Books (Prometheus Press).

Quill, Timothy. 1996. *A Midwife Through the Dying Process: Stories of Healing and Hard Choices at the End of Life*. Baltimore: Johns Hopkins University Press.

——. 1995. "You Promised Me I Wouldn't Die Like This!—A Bad Death as a Medical Emergency." *Archives of Internal Medicine*, 155: 1250–1254.

——. 1993a. *Death and Dignity: Making Choices and Taking Charge*. New York: W. W. Norton.

——. 1993b. "Doctor, I Want To Die. Will You Help Me?" *Journal of the American Medical Association*, 270(7): 870–873.

——. 1991. "Death and Dignity—A Case of Individualized Decision Making." *New England Journal of Medicine*, 324(10): 691–694.

Quill, Timothy, C. Cassel, and D. Meier. 1992. "Care of the Hopelessly Ill—Proposed Clinical Criteria for Physician Assisted Suicide." *New England Journal of Medicine*, 327(19): 1380–1384.

Rachels, James. 1986. *The End of Life: Euthanasia and Morality*. Oxford: Oxford University Press.

Regan, Tom, ed. 1980. *Matters of Life and Death*. Philadelphia: Temple University Press.

Robinson, Wade L., and Michael S. Pritchard, eds. 1979. *Medical Responsibility*. Clifton, N.J.: Humana Press.

Sabatino, Charles. 1993. "Surely the Wizard Will Help Us, Toto? Implementing the Patient Self-Determination Act." *Hastings Center Report*, January/February, 12–16.

Sacks M., and I. Kemperman. 1992. "*Final Exit* as a Manual for Suicide in Depressed Patients." *American Journal of Psychiatry* (Letters), 149(6): 842.

Sandel, Michael. 1997. "The Hard Questions: Last Rights." *The New Republic*, April 14, 27.

Sanders, Stephanie. 1992. "A Time to Live or a Time to Die?" *Nursing Times*, 88(45): 34–36.

Savulescu, Julian. 1994. "Rational Desires and the Limitation of Life-Sustaining Treatment." *Bioethics*, 8(3): 191–222.

Scheper, T., and S. Duursma. 1994. "Euthanasia: The Dutch Experience." *Age and Aging*, 23: 3–8.

Sedler, Robert. 1993. "The Constitution and Hastening Inevitable Death." *Hastings Center Report*, 23(5): 20–25.

Selzer, Richard. 1994. *Raising the Dead*. New York: Whittle/ Viking.

Senate of Canada. 1995. *Of Life and Death: Report of the Special Senate Committee on Euthanasia and Assisted Suicide.* Ottawa: Ministery of Supply and Services.

Seneca. 1969. *Letters from a Stoic.* Letter 77. Trans. Robin Campbell. Baltimore: Penguin Books.

Shapiro, R., A. Derse, M. Gottlieb, D. Schiedermayer, and M. Olson. 1994. "Willingness to Perform Euthanasia: A Survey of Physician Attitudes." *Archives of Internal Medicine,* 154: 575–584.

Shavelson, Lonny. 1995. *A Chosen Death: The Dying Confront Assisted Suicide.* New York: Simon and Schuster.

Shneidman, Edwin. 1996. *The Suicidal Mind.* New York: Oxford University Press.

———. 1993. *Suicide as Psychache: A Clinical Approach to Self-Destructive Behavior.* Northvale, N.J.: Aronson.

———. 1984, *Death: Current Perspectives,* 3rd edition. Mountain View: Mayfield Publishing Co. (Battin, 1982a, doesn't appear in the 1995 4th edition of this anthology.)

———, ed. 1976. *Suicidology: Contemporary Developments.* New York: Grune and Stratton.

———, ed. 1969. *On the Nature of Suicide.* San Francisco: Jossey-Bass.

Silberfeld, Michel, forthcoming. "Vulnerable Persons." *International Journal of Law and Psychiatry.*

———. 1992. "The Use of 'Risk' in Decision-Making." *Canadian Journal of Aging,* 11(2): 124–136.

Silberfeld, Michel, and David Checkland. 1999. "Faulty Judgment, Expert Opinion and Decision-Making Capacity." *Theoretical Medicine and Bioethics."* 20(4): 377–393.

Silberfeld, Michel, and A. Fish. 1994. *When the Mind Fails: A Guide to Dealing with Incompetency.* Toronto: University of Toronto Press.

Silberfeld, Michel, K. Madigan, and B. Dickens. 1994. "Liability Concerns about the Implementation of Advance Directives." *The Canadian Medical Association Journal*, 151(3): 286–289.

Silverstone, P. H., T. Lemay, J. Elliot, V. Hsu, and R. Starko. 1996. "The Prevalence of Major Depressive Disorder and Low Self-Esteem in Medical Patients." *Canadian Journal of Psychiatry*, 41(2): 67–74.

Simpson, Michael A. 1987. *Dying, Death, and Grief: A Critical Bibliography*. Pittsburgh: University of Pittsburgh Press.

——. 1979. *The Facts of Death*. Englewood Cliffs, N.J.: Spectrum/Prentice-Hall.

Southard, Samuel. 1991. *Death and Dying: A Bibliographical Survey*. New York: Greenwood Press.

Spicker, Stuart, Stanley Ingman, and Ian Lawson, eds. 1987. *Ethical Dimensions of Geriatric Care: Value Conflicts for the 21st Century*. Dordrecht, Netherlands: Reidel.

Spicker, Stuart, and R. M. Veatch, eds. 1975. *Death Inside Out*. Hastings Center Report. New York: Harper and Row.

Stillion, Judith M. 1989. *Suicide Across the Life Span—Premature Exits*. New York: Hemisphere Publishing Company.

Stolberg, Sheryl Gay. 1998. "Guide Covers Territory Suicide Law Does Not Explore." *The New York Times*, April 21.

Storch, Janet. 1982. *Patients' Rights: Ethical and Legal Issues in Health Care and Nursing*. Toronto: McGraw-Hill Ryerson Ltd.

Sudnow, David. 1967. *Passing On: The Social Organization of Dying*. Englewood Cliffs, N.J.: Prentice-Hall.

Tallis, Raymond. 1996. "Is There a Slippery Slope?—Arguments For and Against the Various Definitions of Euthanasia." *Medicine*, January, 12.

Teengel, Erwin. 1964. *Suicide and Attempted Suicide*. New York: Penguin Books.

Twycross, Robert G. 1988. *Symptom Control in Terminal Cancer, Lecture Notes*. Oxford: Oxford University Press.

Urofsky, Melvin I., and Philip E. 1996. *The Right to Die: A Two-Volume Anthology of Scholarly Articles*. New York: Garland Publishing.

Van Biema, David. 1997. "Fatal Doses: Assisted Suicide Soars in an Afflicted Community." *Time*, February 17, 53.

van der Burg, Wibren. 1992. "The Slippery-Slope Argument." *The Journal of Clinical Ethics*, 3(4): 256–269.

Van Hoof, Anton. 1960. *From Autothanasia to Suicide: Self Killing in Classical Antiquity*. London: Routledge.

Veatch, Robert M. 1995. "Abandoning Informed Consent." *Hastings Center Report*, 25(2): 5–12.

——. 1989. *Death, Dying and the Biological Revolution: Our Last Quest for Responsibility*. New Haven and London: Yale University Press.

——. 1981. *A Theory of Medical Ethics*. New York: Basic Books.

Wal, G., and R. Dillman. 1994. "Euthanasia in the Netherlands." *British Medical Journal*, 308: 1346–1349.

Walton, Douglas N. 1979. *On Defining Death: An Analytic Study of the Concept of Death in Philosophy and Medical Ethics*. Montreal: McGill-Queen's University Press.

Wass, Hannalore, Felix Berardo, and Robert Neimeyer, eds. 1987. *Dying: Facing the Facts*. 2nd edition. New York: Hemisphere.

Watts, D., and T. Howell. 1992. "Assisted Suicide Is Not Voluntary Active Euthanasia." *Journal of the American Geriatrics Society*, 40(10): 1043–1046.

Weir, Robert F. 1997. *Physician-Assisted Suicide*. Bloomington: Indiana University Press.

——. 1992. "The Morality of Physician-Assisted Suicide." *Law Medicine and Health Care*, 20(1–2): 116–126.

Wennberg, Robert N. 1989. *Terminal Choices: Euthanasia, Suicide, and the Right to Die*. Grand Rapids, Mich.: Eerdman's.

Werth, J. L., and B. J. Liddle. 1994. "Psychotherapists' Attitudes Toward Rational Suicide." *Psychotherapy*, 31(3): 440–448.

Wilks, I. 1997. "The Debate Over Risk-Related Standards of Competence." *Bioethics*, 11(5): 413–426.

Young, E., and S. Jex. 1992. "The Patient Self-Determination Act: Potential Ethical Quandries and Benefits." *Cambridge Quarterly of Healthcare Ethics*, 2: 107–115.

The World Wide Web

Links to many Websites offering relevant material may be found on the Internet. Yahoo! is a good place to start searching (www.yahoo.com). Other useful search engines are Excite (www.excite.com) and AltaVista (www.altavista.digital.com). One of the sites available from Yahoo! is the Euthanasia World Directory on the World Wide Web. Another interesting site is *The New York Times* forum (forums.nytimes.com). Note that Web addresses change fairly often but can usually be tracked down through Yahoo!, Excite, AltaVista and other search engines.

THE CONTRIBUTORS

Margaret P. Battin, Professor of Philosophy and Adjunct Professor of Internal Medicine, Division of Medical Ethics, University of Utah. She holds an M.F.A. from Bryn Mawr and a Ph.D. from the University of California at Irvine. The author of prize-winning short stories, she has authored, edited or co-edited 12 books, among them a study of philosophical issues in suicide, a collection on age-rationing of medical care and a text on professional ethics. *The Least Worst Death* is a collection of essays on end-of-life issues written over the last 15 years. She is engaged in research on active euthanasia and assisted suicide in the Netherlands and recently published *Ethical Issues in Suicide*, trade-titled *The Death Debate*, as well as several coedited collections, including *Drug Use in Euthanasia and Assisted Suicide* and *Physician-Assisted Suicide: Expanding the Debate*. Published in 1999, *Praying for a Cure* is a jointly authored volume on the ethics of religious refusal of medical treatment. She is currently writing a book on world population growth and reproductive rights, and a sourcebook on ethical issues in suicide.

Robert Wesley Boston, M.D., F.R.C.P. (C), trained in pediatrics at the Royal College of Physicians and Surgeons (Canada) and in neonatology at the Harvard Medical School and London's University College Hospital. He established and headed the Neonatology program at the Kingston General Hospital

(Ont.), and was Professor and Head of Pediatrics before re-training in Palliative Medicine in Montreal and in British Hospices in London, Edinburgh and other centers. He initiated and headed the Palliative Care Program at the Kingston General Hospital.

David Checkland, Ph.D., is Associate Professor of Philosophy at Ryerson Polytechnic University. Formerly he served as the ethicist at the Competency Clinic at the Baycrest Centre for Geriatric Care, Department of Psychiatry (Toronto, Ont.). He has published numerous articles on decisional capacity (many with Michel Silberfeld), and is coeditor (with James Wong) of *Thinking About Teen Parenting* (forthcoming, University of Toronto Press).

Eike-Henner W. Kluge, is Professor and Chair of the Department of Philosophy at the University of Victoria (B.C.). He has published five books, including the first medical-ethics text for Canadian physicians, and more than 40 articles in biomedical ethics. He was founding Director of the Department of Ethics and Legal Affairs of the Canadian Medical Association. He served as the first expert witness in medical ethics recognized by Canadian courts. He has acted in that capacity in Ontario, British Columbia and Alberta. He was the ethics consultant in the Sue Rodriguez case.

Anne Mullens, is a Canadian journalist and author who specializes in medical issues. She is the author of two critically acclaimed books, *Missed Conceptions* (McGraw Hill, 1990), about infertility and reproductive technologies, and *Timely Death* (Knopf, 1996), about euthanasia and assisted suicide. *Timely Death* won the 1996 Edna Staebler Award for Creative Non-Fiction. She lives in Victoria (B.C.).

Jan Narveson, Ph.D., is Professor of Philosophy at the University of Waterloo (Ont.). His extensive writings on moral and political philosophy include many articles, as well as *Morality and Utility* (1967), *The Libertarian Idea* (1988), *Moral Matters* (1993) and (with Marilyn Friedman) *Political Correctness: For and Against* (1995).

C. G. Prado, Ph.D., is Professor of Philosophy at Queen's University (Kingston, Ont.). His publications include *Starting with Foucault: An Introduction to Genealogy*; *Assisted Suicide: Theory and Practice in Elective Death* (with S. J. Taylor); *Descartes and Foucault: A Contrastive Introduction to Philosophy*; *The Last Choice: Preemptive Suicide in Advanced Age*; *The Limits of Pragmatism*; *Rethinking How We Age: A New View of the Aging Mind*; *Making Believe: Philosophical Reflections on Fiction*; and *Illusions of Faith: A Critique of Noncredal Religion*.

Russell Savage, Ph.D., LL.B., is presently serving in the Calgary office of Alberta Justice, Criminal Division. He has conducted prosecutions at all levels of Court in Alberta. He is also active in legal education in the Calgary legal community. For the past year he has been seconded as Alberta Justice Representative to CLASS.ab.ca Inc., an innovative legal database for criminal lawyers in Alberta and across Canada.

Michel Silberfeld, M.D., M.Sc., is the Coordinator of the Competency Clinic at the Baycrest Centre for Geriatric Care, Department of Psychiatry (Toronto, Ont.). He has published extensively on the subject of mental capacity, and is coauthor (with Arthur Fish) of *When the Mind Fails: A Guide to Dealing with Incompetency* (University of Toronto Press).

Bronwyn Singleton, M.A., completed a graduate program in philosophy at Queen's University (Kingston, Ont.) in 1998, having done her undergraduate work at the University of Western Ontario (London, Ont.). She currently lives and works in Toronto (Ont.).

Sandra J. Taylor, Ph.D., is currently the Bioethicist and Director of Ethics Education in the Faculty of Health Sciences at Queen's University (Kingston, Ont.). She is also the Clinical Ethicist at the Kingston General Hospital. Additionally, she holds appointments in the Departments of Family Medicine, Nursing and Philosophy.

Printed and bound
in Boucherville, Quebec, Canada by
MARC VEILLEUX IMPRIMEUR INC.
in April, 2000